Mysterious Conspiracies: The Secret Plots of History

Shah Rukh

Published by Shah Rukh, 2024.

While every precaution has been taken in the preparation of this book, the publisher assumes no responsibility for errors or omissions, or for damages resulting from the use of the information contained herein.

MYSTERIOUS CONSPIRACIES: THE SECRET PLOTS OF HISTORY

First edition. July 4, 2024.

Copyright © 2024 Shah Rukh.

Written by Shah Rukh.

Table of Contents

Prologue

History is often written by the victors, and with it comes a tapestry of narratives that shape our understanding of the past. Yet, lurking in the shadows of documented events are stories that challenge the very fabric of our accepted history—stories of mysterious conspiracies, clandestine plots, and secret machinations that whisper of truths obscured and realities manipulated.

Welcome to "Mysterious Conspiracies: The Secret Plots of History," a journey through some of the most enigmatic and perplexing conspiracies that have captivated the human imagination for decades, even centuries. From the chilling accounts of unexplained disappearances to the intricate webs spun by powerful secret societies, this book delves into the hidden corners of history where mystery reigns and facts blur into conjecture.

In these pages, you will encounter tales that question the official versions of significant historical events, shed light on shadowy organizations operating behind the scenes, and explore the strange coincidences that defy rational explanation. Each chapter is a window into a different conspiracy, meticulously researched and presented to offer you, the reader, a glimpse into the unknown.

As you embark on this exploration, keep an open mind and a discerning eye. While some may dismiss these stories as mere speculation or fanciful fiction, others might find kernels of truth that provoke deeper thought and curiosity. In the end, the allure of these conspiracies lies not only in the mysteries they present but also in the questions they raise about power, knowledge, and the very nature of truth.

Are these conspiracies the products of overactive imaginations, or do they point to hidden realities that authorities would prefer remain concealed? The answer, dear reader, is yours to ponder as you navigate the labyrinth of secrets contained within this book.

Prepare to question, wonder, and perhaps even doubt the histories you thought you knew. The journey through "Mysterious Conspiracies: The Secret Plots of History" promises to be as enlightening as it is unsettling. Let the exploration of the unknown begin.

2

Chapter 1: The Roswell Incident

The Roswell Incident remains one of the most enduring and controversial events in the history of UFO phenomena, conspiracy theories, and governmental secrecy. It all began in early July 1947, when a mysterious object crashed on a ranch near Roswell, New Mexico. The official story by the United States military initially claimed it was a "flying disc," but within hours, this was retracted and replaced with an explanation that it was merely a weather balloon. This sudden shift in the narrative sparked a wave of speculation and doubt, laying the groundwork for a conspiracy theory that has persisted for decades.

The timeline of events is crucial to understanding the Roswell Incident's impact and the subsequent conspiracy theories. On July 8, 1947, the Roswell Army Air Field (RAAF) issued a press release stating that they had recovered a "flying disc" from a ranch near Roswell. This announcement was widely covered by the media, creating a sensation. However, later that same day, another statement was released, this time from the higher authorities of the Eighth Air Force at Fort Worth, Texas, clarifying that the recovered debris was not a "flying disc" but a weather balloon carrying a radar target. The debris was shown to the press, and the story seemingly concluded.

However, the swift change in the official narrative raised suspicions. Many began to question why the military would initially describe the debris as a "flying disc" if it were merely a weather balloon. Witnesses, including rancher W.W. "Mack" Brazel, who discovered the debris, reported that the material found was unlike anything they had ever seen, with descriptions of thin, flexible metallic sheets that could not be damaged. Additionally, some accounts mentioned the presence of strange hieroglyphic-like symbols on the debris.

In the years following the incident, interest waned until the late 1970s, when UFO researchers Stanton Friedman and William Moore reignited the controversy. Their investigations, along with testimonies from new witnesses, suggested a cover-up by the government. Jesse Marcel, an intelligence officer at the RAAF who was involved in the initial recovery, publicly stated that the material he handled was not from any known weather balloon but something far more advanced and possibly extraterrestrial.

The resurgence of interest in the Roswell Incident led to numerous books, documentaries, and articles exploring various theories. One of the most compelling pieces of evidence presented by UFO researchers was the claim that the debris recovered was part of a top-secret military project named "Project Mogul." This project involved high-altitude balloons equipped with microphones to detect Soviet nuclear tests. The materials used in Project Mogul, including the radar reflectors and other components, matched the descriptions of the Roswell debris, providing a plausible explanation that did not involve extraterrestrials.

Despite the Project Mogul explanation, many still believe that something more extraordinary occurred at Roswell. Conspiracy theories abound, with some claiming that the government recovered not just debris but also alien bodies. These theories were fueled by supposed deathbed confessions, leaked documents, and testimonies from individuals claiming inside knowledge. One particularly sensational claim came from a retired mortician named Glenn Dennis, who stated that he was involved in the autopsies of alien bodies at the Roswell Army Air Field hospital.

The U.S. government has made several attempts to debunk the Roswell conspiracy theories. In the 1990s, the Air Force released two reports addressing the incident. The first report, published in 1994, reiterated the Project Mogul explanation for the debris. The second report, released in 1997, aimed to explain the claims of alien bodies by suggesting that witnesses had seen crash test dummies used in high-altitude parachute tests, which were mistaken for extraterrestrials due to their unusual appearance and the passage of time distorting memories.

Despite these official explanations, the Roswell Incident continues to captivate the public imagination. It has become a cornerstone of UFO lore and conspiracy culture, symbolizing a distrust of government and a fascination with the possibility of extraterrestrial life. The incident has inspired countless fictional works, from movies and TV shows to novels and video games, embedding itself deeply in popular culture.

The legacy of the Roswell Incident is multifaceted. On one hand, it has led to serious scientific inquiry into the possibility of extraterrestrial life and the study of unidentified aerial phenomena (UAPs). On the other hand, it has also spawned a plethora of conspiracy theories that often lack credible evidence but persist due to their compelling narratives and the human tendency to distrust official accounts. Roswell has also become a tourist attraction, with the town hosting an annual UFO festival and the International UFO Museum and Research Center, drawing visitors from around the world who are eager to explore the mystery firsthand.

The Roswell Incident illustrates the power of narrative and the enduring human quest for answers to profound mysteries. Whether it was a case of mistaken identity involving a secret military project or a genuine encounter with something otherworldly, the incident has left an indelible mark on the collective consciousness. It serves as a reminder of how a single event, shrouded in ambiguity and secrecy, can spark a chain reaction of speculation, investigation, and belief that spans generations.

As new technologies and declassified documents continue to emerge, the Roswell Incident remains a focal point for those seeking the truth about UFOs and government transparency. While definitive proof of extraterrestrial involvement remains elusive, the ongoing interest in Roswell ensures that the debate will continue, blending science, skepticism, and wonder in a complex tapestry of human curiosity and imagination.

Chapter 2: The Moon Landing Hoax

The Moon Landing Hoax theory, one of the most persistent and widely debated conspiracy theories, asserts that the Apollo moon landings were staged by NASA and the United States government. Proponents of this theory argue that the six manned moon landings between 1969 and 1972 were elaborate fabrications, designed to assert U.S. dominance in the Space Race during the Cold War era. This theory gained traction shortly after the first moon landing, with various individuals and groups presenting what they claim to be evidence of a hoax.

The context of the Apollo moon landings is crucial to understanding why the hoax theory emerged. During the 1960s, the United States and the Soviet Union were engaged in a fierce competition for space exploration supremacy. This rivalry was a key component of the Cold War, with both nations seeking to demonstrate their technological and ideological superiority. In 1961, President John F. Kennedy famously declared that the U.S. would land a man on the moon before the end of the decade, setting the stage for an ambitious and costly space program.

NASA's Apollo program, which eventually succeeded in landing astronauts on the moon, was an enormous undertaking that involved the efforts of tens of thousands of scientists, engineers, and technicians. The first successful moon landing occurred on July 20, 1969, when Apollo 11 astronauts Neil Armstrong and Buzz Aldrin set foot on the lunar surface. Armstrong's words, "That's one small step for man, one giant leap for mankind," became iconic, and the event was broadcast live to millions around the world. However, almost immediately, some began to question the authenticity of the moon landings.

The moon landing hoax theory rests on several main arguments, each of which has been thoroughly debunked by experts but continues to be cited by conspiracy theorists. One of the most common claims is that the photographs and videos from the moon landings contain anomalies that suggest they were filmed on a soundstage. For instance, skeptics point to the lack of stars in the lunar sky, the behavior of the American flag, and the peculiar shadows and lighting in the images. They argue that these anomalies indicate the use of artificial lighting and backdrops.

The absence of stars in the moon landing photographs is easily explained by the limitations of the camera equipment used. The cameras were set to capture the brightly lit lunar surface, which required short exposure times that would not pick up the faint light of distant stars. Similarly, the behavior of the American flag, which appears to be waving, is attributed to the fact that it was designed with a horizontal rod to keep it extended. The flag's movement occurred when astronauts planted it into the lunar soil, and it continued to oscillate due to the lack of atmospheric resistance on the moon.

Another argument posed by moon landing hoax proponents involves the shadows in the lunar images. They claim that the shadows appear to be inconsistent, suggesting the use of multiple light sources. In reality, the shadows can be explained by the uneven terrain of the moon's surface and the single light source—the sun—casting shadows at various angles. The reflective properties of the lunar soil also contribute to the appearance of the shadows, creating complex lighting effects.

Some conspiracy theorists also assert that the technology available in the 1960s was insufficient to safely send humans to the moon and back. They argue that the radiation in the Van Allen belts, which encircle the Earth, would have been lethal to astronauts. However, NASA carefully planned the trajectories of the Apollo missions to minimize exposure to the radiation, and the spacecraft were equipped with adequate shielding. The duration of exposure was short enough to prevent significant harm to the astronauts.

The hoax theory also posits that the Soviet Union, which closely monitored the U.S. space program, would have exposed any deception. Given the intense rivalry between the two superpowers, it is highly unlikely that the Soviet Union would have remained silent if they had evidence of a hoax. In fact, the Soviet space agency tracked the Apollo missions and congratulated the U.S. on its success, lending credibility to the authenticity of the moon landings.

In addition to these technical arguments, the moon landing hoax theory is fueled by a broader distrust of government and authority. The 1960s and 1970s were a time of significant social and political upheaval in the United States, marked by events such as the Vietnam War and the Watergate scandal. This climate of skepticism made some people more receptive to the idea that the government could orchestrate a massive deception.

One of the most influential works promoting the moon landing hoax theory is the book "We Never Went to the Moon: America's Thirty Billion Dollar Swindle" by Bill Kaysing, published in 1976. Kaysing, a former technical writer for Rocketdyne, a company involved in the Apollo program, claimed that the moon landings were staged and that he had inside knowledge of the cover-up. Although Kaysing's assertions were based on speculation and lacked credible evidence, his book helped to popularize the hoax theory.

The moon landing hoax theory gained further attention in the late 1990s and early 2000s with the advent of the internet, which allowed conspiracy theories to spread more rapidly. Websites, forums, and social media platforms provided a fertile ground for proponents of the hoax theory to share their ideas and attract new followers. Television programs and documentaries, such as the 2001 Fox special "Conspiracy Theory: Did We Land on the Moon?" also contributed to the theory's visibility, presenting misleading and cherry-picked information that fueled public curiosity and doubt.

Despite the persistence of the moon landing hoax theory, there is overwhelming evidence supporting the reality of the Apollo missions. This evidence includes the physical samples of lunar rock brought back by the astronauts, which have been studied and confirmed to be of extraterrestrial origin. The missions were also tracked by independent observatories and amateur radio operators worldwide, who received transmissions from the Apollo spacecraft. Furthermore, recent lunar missions by other countries, such as China's Chang'e program, have provided high-resolution images of the Apollo landing sites, showing the remnants of the lunar modules and the astronauts' footprints.

NASA has repeatedly addressed the hoax claims, providing detailed explanations and evidence to counter the conspiracy theories. In addition to scientific and technical rebuttals, the agency has emphasized the human aspect of the Apollo program, highlighting the dedication and bravery of the astronauts, engineers, and scientists who made the moon landings possible. The legacy of the Apollo missions continues to inspire new generations of scientists, engineers, and explorers, who view the achievements of the 1960s and 1970s as a testament to human ingenuity and perseverance.

The moon landing hoax theory, while debunked and discredited by experts, persists as a cultural phenomenon. It reflects broader themes of skepticism, mistrust, and the appeal of alternative narratives that challenge official accounts. The theory serves as a reminder of the importance of critical thinking, scientific literacy, and the need to scrutinize sources of information. As long as there are unanswered questions and unexplored mysteries, conspiracy theories like the moon landing hoax will continue to capture the imagination and provoke debate.

Chapter 3: The Illuminati Agenda

The Illuminati Agenda is one of the most enduring and elaborate conspiracy theories in modern history. The idea of the Illuminati originated in the late 18th century with the founding of a secret society called the Bavarian Illuminati, established by Adam Weishaupt in 1776. This organization aimed to promote Enlightenment ideals and secularism, advocating for freedom of thought and the separation of church and state. However, the original Illuminati was short-lived, disbanded and suppressed by the Bavarian government within a decade. Despite this, the myth of the Illuminati persisted and evolved, morphing into a complex narrative that suggests a hidden elite controls world events and seeks to establish a New World Order.

The Illuminati conspiracy theory posits that a clandestine group of powerful individuals or families exerts immense influence over global affairs, including politics, economics, media, and culture. According to proponents, this secret cabal aims to create a one-world government, eliminating national boundaries and individual freedoms. This agenda allegedly involves manipulating major events, controlling institutions, and perpetuating conflicts to consolidate their power. The theory often links the Illuminati to various historical and contemporary figures, from politicians and business leaders to celebrities and intellectuals.

One of the foundational aspects of the Illuminati Agenda theory is the belief that this secret society operates through infiltration and manipulation. Conspiracy theorists argue that the Illuminati has embedded itself within influential organizations and governments, subtly steering policies and decisions to further their goals. This idea of covert control extends to the financial sector, where the Illuminati is thought to manipulate global markets, control central banks, and orchestrate economic crises to maintain dominance and control over resources.

Central to the Illuminati Agenda is the concept of the New World Order, a supposed plan to centralize global governance under a single, authoritarian regime. This idea gained significant traction during the 20th century, particularly in the wake of global conflicts and the establishment of international organizations such as the United Nations. Conspiracy theorists interpret efforts toward global cooperation and integration as steps toward this ultimate goal, viewing treaties, economic unions, and multinational corporations as tools of the Illuminati.

The cultural impact of the Illuminati Agenda theory is profound, influencing various forms of media and public discourse. Books, films, music, and television shows have all drawn upon Illuminati symbolism and themes, either to critique perceived power structures or to sensationalize the conspiracy. Symbols such as the all-seeing eye, the pyramid, and the pentagram are often cited as evidence of the Illuminati's presence and influence. These symbols are believed to be hidden in plain sight, subtly conditioning the public and signaling the power of the Illuminati.

One notable aspect of the Illuminati Agenda theory is its adaptability and ability to incorporate new events and figures. Whenever a significant global event occurs, from political upheavals to natural disasters, proponents of the theory often interpret it as part of the Illuminati's plan. This ability to evolve and absorb various elements has allowed the theory to persist and remain relevant across different eras and cultural contexts.

The Illuminati Agenda theory frequently intersects with other conspiracy theories, creating a web of interconnected beliefs. For instance, the theory often overlaps with ideas about secret societies like the Freemasons, the Skull and Bones society, and the Bilderberg Group. Additionally, it aligns with theories about mind control, such as MK-Ultra, and technological surveillance, like the widespread use of data collection and monitoring by governments and corporations.

These connections create a comprehensive narrative that portrays a vast, interconnected network of control and manipulation.

A significant challenge in addressing the Illuminati Agenda theory is its reliance on circumstantial evidence and interpretative reasoning. Proponents often point to coincidences, anomalies, and patterns in historical and contemporary events as proof of the Illuminati's influence. They argue that these pieces of evidence, when viewed collectively, reveal a hidden agenda. Critics, however, emphasize that correlation does not imply causation and that the theory often lacks concrete, verifiable evidence. This difference in interpretation highlights the broader issue of how individuals perceive and process information, particularly in an era of abundant and often contradictory data.

The internet has played a crucial role in the dissemination and perpetuation of the Illuminati Agenda theory. Online forums, social media platforms, and video-sharing websites have provided spaces for conspiracy theorists to share ideas, build communities, and attract new followers. The viral nature of online content means that Illuminati-related theories and symbols can quickly spread, reaching a wide audience. This digital environment also fosters a sense of confirmation bias, as individuals are more likely to encounter information that reinforces their existing beliefs.

Psychologically, the appeal of the Illuminati Agenda theory can be attributed to several factors. It offers a simple explanation for complex and often chaotic global events, providing a sense of order and understanding. It also taps into a deep-seated mistrust of authority and institutions, which has been exacerbated by real instances of corruption, deception, and abuse of power. Additionally, the theory provides a sense of empowerment and purpose, as believers see themselves as part of a knowledgeable group that has uncovered the "truth" about the world.

From a sociological perspective, the Illuminati Agenda theory reflects broader anxieties about globalization, technological change, and the erosion of traditional structures. In an increasingly interconnected and complex world, the idea of a shadowy elite pulling the strings can be a compelling narrative that explains feelings of powerlessness and disorientation. The theory also serves as a form of social critique, highlighting concerns about inequality, surveillance, and the concentration of power.

Despite its persistence, the Illuminati Agenda theory faces significant criticism and debunking from scholars, journalists, and experts. Investigative research has shown that many of the claims made by proponents are based on misinterpretations, exaggerations, and fabrications. Historical analysis reveals that the original Bavarian Illuminati was a relatively small and short-lived group, with no evidence of its continuation or evolution into a global conspiracy. Scientific and rational inquiry emphasizes the importance of critical thinking and skepticism in evaluating extraordinary claims.

The legacy of the Illuminati Agenda theory is complex. On one hand, it represents a significant strand of contemporary folklore, reflecting enduring themes of secrecy, power, and resistance. On the other hand, it can contribute to misinformation, paranoia, and division, diverting attention from real issues and undermining trust in legitimate institutions. Understanding the Illuminati Agenda theory involves exploring the interplay between history, culture, psychology, and technology, recognizing the ways in which narratives of power and control resonate with human experiences and fears.

Chapter 4: The Assassination of JFK

The assassination of President John F. Kennedy on November 22, 1963, stands as one of the most significant and scrutinized events in American history. The tragedy occurred in Dallas, Texas, as Kennedy rode in an open-top convertible through Dealey Plaza. The events that unfolded that day, and the subsequent investigations, have fueled countless conspiracy theories, debates, and controversies that continue to capture the public imagination over half a century later.

The day began with President Kennedy and First Lady Jacqueline Kennedy arriving in Dallas as part of a campaign tour aimed at garnering support for the upcoming 1964 election. They were accompanied by Texas Governor John Connally and his wife, Nellie, who were also in the motorcade. As the motorcade made its way through downtown Dallas, it was greeted by enthusiastic crowds. The route took a turn onto Elm Street, passing the Texas School Book Depository, where at 12:30 p.m., shots rang out.

Kennedy was struck by two bullets: one that passed through his neck and a fatal shot that struck his head. Governor Connally was also seriously injured by another bullet. The motorcade rushed to Parkland Memorial Hospital, but despite the efforts of the medical staff, President Kennedy was pronounced dead at 1:00 p.m. The nation was plunged into shock and mourning, as news of the assassination spread rapidly.

In the immediate aftermath, attention quickly turned to finding the perpetrator. Within hours, Lee Harvey Oswald, a former Marine who had previously defected to the Soviet Union and returned to the United States, was arrested. Oswald worked at the Texas School Book Depository and was seen leaving the building shortly after the shooting. He was charged with the murder of President Kennedy and a Dallas police officer, J.D. Tippit, who was killed shortly after the assassination. Oswald denied the charges, claiming he was a "patsy," and maintained his innocence.

Two days later, on November 24, 1963, Oswald was shot and killed by nightclub owner Jack Ruby while being transferred from the city jail to the county jail. Ruby's actions, captured live on television, added another layer of mystery and conspiracy to the unfolding drama. Ruby claimed he killed Oswald out of grief and anger over Kennedy's death, but his motives have been the subject of speculation and doubt.

To address the public's demand for answers, President Lyndon B. Johnson established the Warren Commission on November 29, 1963, chaired by Chief Justice Earl Warren. The commission's mandate was to investigate the circumstances surrounding Kennedy's assassination. After nearly a year of investigation, the Warren Commission released its report in September 1964, concluding that Lee Harvey Oswald acted alone in assassinating President Kennedy. The commission also determined that there was no evidence of a conspiracy involving Oswald and that Jack Ruby had no ties to any larger plot.

Despite the Warren Commission's findings, doubts and suspicions persisted. Critics pointed to perceived inconsistencies and unanswered questions in the commission's report. The single-bullet theory, which posited that one bullet caused multiple wounds to both Kennedy and Connally, was particularly controversial and widely debated. Skeptics argued that the theory was implausible and that it was more likely that multiple gunmen were involved.

The Zapruder film, a home movie shot by Abraham Zapruder that captured the assassination, became a crucial piece of evidence. The film's graphic depiction of the fatal headshot to Kennedy intensified public fascination and skepticism. Some claimed that the film showed evidence of a second shooter, possibly from the grassy knoll area to the right of the motorcade. This theory was bolstered by eyewitness accounts that reported hearing shots from different directions.

Over the years, numerous alternative theories about Kennedy's assassination have emerged. These theories implicate various entities, including the CIA, the Mafia, anti-Castro Cuban exiles, and even elements within the U.S. government. One popular theory suggests that Kennedy was targeted because of his administration's stance on civil rights, the Cold War, and efforts to limit the power of the CIA and the military-industrial complex.

In 1976, in response to growing public skepticism and new information, the U.S. House of Representatives established the House Select Committee on Assassinations (HSCA) to reexamine the evidence. The HSCA's final report, published in 1979, concluded that Kennedy was "probably assassinated as a result of a conspiracy." The committee based this conclusion on acoustic evidence from a police dictabelt recording that appeared to indicate multiple gunshots. However, this finding was later disputed by the National Academy of Sciences, which questioned the validity of the acoustic analysis.

The release of previously classified documents over the decades has provided new insights but also fueled further speculation. The JFK Records Act of 1992 mandated the declassification of thousands of documents related to the assassination. While these documents have shed light on various aspects of the investigation, they have not definitively resolved the lingering questions. The release of additional documents in 2017 and 2018 continued this trend, offering more information but no clear answers.

Several individuals and researchers have dedicated their lives to investigating the Kennedy assassination, each contributing to the extensive body of literature on the subject. Books, documentaries, and movies have explored the events from multiple perspectives, often reaching different conclusions. Oliver Stone's 1991 film "JFK" popularized many conspiracy theories and reignited public interest, prompting renewed calls for further investigation and transparency.

One aspect that adds to the complexity of the Kennedy assassination is the involvement of key figures and organizations with their own contentious histories. For example, Oswald's time in the Soviet Union and his connections to pro-Castro and anti-Castro groups have led to various theories about foreign involvement. Additionally, Jack Ruby's ties to organized crime and his seemingly inexplicable decision to kill Oswald have fueled speculation about a Mafia connection.

The assassination also had profound and lasting impacts on American politics and society. Kennedy's death marked a turning point, ushering in a period of political turmoil and social upheaval. The loss of a charismatic and inspiring leader left a void, and the subsequent escalation of the Vietnam War and the civil rights movement further polarized the nation. The assassination contributed to a growing mistrust of government and institutions, a sentiment that has only deepened over time.

The legacy of the Kennedy assassination extends beyond the events of November 22, 1963. It serves as a cautionary tale about the vulnerabilities of public figures and the potential for unforeseen consequences. The persistent questions and theories surrounding the assassination reflect broader anxieties about power, secrecy, and accountability. As long as there are unanswered questions and unexplained aspects, the fascination with JFK's assassination will continue.

In recent years, technological advancements and new investigative techniques have provided opportunities to reexamine the evidence with fresh perspectives. Digital analysis of the Zapruder film, ballistic tests, and forensic reconstructions have offered new insights, though no definitive answers. The ongoing pursuit of truth underscores the enduring significance of Kennedy's assassination and its impact on American history and culture.

The assassination of President John F. Kennedy remains one of the most thoroughly investigated and debated events in modern history. The initial findings of the Warren Commission, the subsequent investigations by the HSCA, and the relentless efforts of researchers and conspiracy theorists have all contributed to a complex and multifaceted narrative. While the official conclusion is that Lee Harvey Oswald acted alone, the enduring doubts and alternative theories ensure that the debate will continue. The search for truth, driven by a desire for closure and understanding, reflects the broader human quest to make sense of pivotal and traumatic events.

Chapter 5: The Death of Marilyn Monroe

The death of Marilyn Monroe on August 5, 1962, remains one of Hollywood's most enduring mysteries, marked by numerous conspiracy theories and widespread speculation. Officially ruled a probable suicide due to acute barbiturate poisoning, Monroe's untimely demise at the age of 36 has inspired endless debates about the circumstances leading to her death, involving figures from the highest echelons of power, including the Kennedy brothers, organized crime figures, and Hollywood elites.

Marilyn Monroe, born Norma Jeane Mortenson, became an icon of the 20th century, known for her beauty, charisma, and talent. Rising from a difficult childhood marked by foster homes and orphanages, she achieved stardom in the 1950s with films like "Gentlemen Prefer Blondes" and "Some Like It Hot." Despite her public persona as a glamorous, carefree star, Monroe struggled with personal issues, including mental health problems, substance abuse, and tumultuous relationships. These struggles often overshadowed her professional achievements and contributed to the tragic narrative surrounding her life and death.

The official account of Monroe's death states that she was found dead in her Brentwood, Los Angeles home by her psychiatrist, Dr. Ralph Greenson, and her housekeeper, Eunice Murray. The police were called to the scene around 4:25 a.m. on August 5, 1962. According to the coroner's report, Monroe had ingested a lethal dose of barbiturates, specifically Nembutal and chloral hydrate. The absence of any signs of external violence led the authorities to conclude that her death was a suicide. However, several inconsistencies and peculiarities in the official narrative have fueled speculation and conspiracy theories over the years.

One of the most persistent theories involves Monroe's alleged relationships with President John F. Kennedy and his brother, Attorney

General Robert F. Kennedy. Rumors of Monroe's romantic involvement with both Kennedys have been a source of intrigue and speculation. Some conspiracy theorists suggest that Monroe's death was orchestrated to prevent her from revealing sensitive information about the Kennedys or other powerful individuals. These theories are bolstered by claims that Monroe was wiretapped and kept under surveillance, and that her house was frequently visited by individuals associated with the Kennedys.

Several authors and researchers have delved into the potential political ramifications of Monroe's relationships with the Kennedys. One theory posits that Monroe possessed knowledge of highly classified information, including details about the United States' dealings with Cuba and the Soviet Union. According to this theory, Monroe's potential to expose these secrets made her a liability, prompting those in power to silence her. Supporters of this theory point to alleged inconsistencies in the timeline of events on the night of her death, the disappearance of her phone records, and conflicting testimonies from those close to her.

Another significant thread in the conspiracy theories surrounding Monroe's death involves her connections to organized crime. During the late 1950s and early 1960s, the mafia wielded considerable influence in Hollywood, and Monroe reportedly had associations with figures linked to organized crime. Some theories suggest that Monroe's death was a result of her involvement with mobsters, who might have seen her as a threat due to her connections with the Kennedys. There are claims that the mafia used Monroe as leverage in their dealings with the political elite, and that her death was a calculated move in their power struggles.

Additionally, some conspiracy theories focus on Monroe's relationship with Dr. Ralph Greenson, her psychiatrist, and other members of her medical team. Monroe was known to be heavily medicated, with prescriptions for various barbiturates and other drugs from multiple doctors. This led to speculation that her death could have been an accidental overdose caused by the negligence or even intentional actions of her medical providers. Critics argue that Monroe was overmedicated and that the combination of drugs she was taking could have created a dangerous situation. There are also claims that Greenson and others might have been complicit in her death, either knowingly or through gross negligence.

The role of Eunice Murray, Monroe's housekeeper, also invites scrutiny. On the night of Monroe's death, Murray's actions and statements raised eyebrows. According to her account, she noticed Monroe's bedroom light on around midnight and called Greenson, who arrived and broke a window to gain access to the room. However, some accounts suggest that Murray was evasive and inconsistent in her statements to the police, leading to suspicions that she might have been coerced or involved in a cover-up. Moreover, the delay in calling the authorities has been cited as suspicious, as it is unclear why Murray or Greenson did not immediately seek medical help when they first noticed something was wrong.

The circumstances of Monroe's autopsy and the handling of her body also contribute to the cloud of mystery surrounding her death. There are reports that crucial organs, including her stomach and intestines, were missing from the autopsy, raising questions about the thoroughness and integrity of the examination. Some theorists argue that this could indicate a deliberate effort to obscure the true cause of death. Additionally, the toxicology report revealed a high concentration of barbiturates in Monroe's system, but no evidence of pills or residue in her stomach, leading to speculation that she might have been administered the drugs through an injection or enema, rather than ingesting them orally.

In the decades since Monroe's death, numerous books, documentaries, and articles have explored the various theories and evidence, each presenting different interpretations of the available information. Some of the most notable works include Norman Mailer's "Marilyn: A Biography," which suggested the involvement of the Kennedys; Anthony Summers' "Goddess: The Secret Lives of Marilyn Monroe," which provided a comprehensive investigation into the possible conspiracies; and Donald Spoto's "Marilyn Monroe: The Biography," which argued for the likelihood of an accidental overdose. These works, along with many others, have kept the debate alive and ensured that Monroe's death remains a topic of fascination and controversy.

Despite the passage of time, new information and perspectives continue to emerge, keeping the case in the public eye. In recent years, previously classified documents and recordings have been released, offering fresh insights into the possible surveillance and monitoring of Monroe. These revelations have added new layers to the theories about her death, suggesting that she was indeed under close scrutiny by various entities, including the FBI and the CIA. This surveillance might have been motivated by her relationships with the Kennedys, her political sympathies, or her associations with individuals deemed to be security risks.

The cultural impact of Marilyn Monroe's death is profound, reflecting broader themes of fame, power, vulnerability, and the darker side of Hollywood. Monroe's life story, marked by her rise to stardom, personal struggles, and tragic end, embodies the complexities of the American Dream. Her death serves as a cautionary tale about the pressures of fame and the potential for exploitation and betrayal in the pursuit of success. It also underscores the societal fascination with celebrity and the public's insatiable curiosity about the private lives of stars.

Monroe's enduring legacy is evident in the continued interest in her life and death. She remains an iconic figure, symbolizing both the allure and the pitfalls of fame. Her image is ubiquitous, adorning posters, books, and memorabilia, and she is frequently referenced in popular culture. The mystery surrounding her death has ensured that she remains a subject of fascination, with each new generation discovering and reinterpreting her story.

24

Chapter 6: The Bermuda Triangle Mysteries

The Bermuda Triangle, known as the Devil's Triangle, is a region in the western part of the North Atlantic Ocean, roughly bounded by Miami, Bermuda, and Puerto Rico. Over the years, this area has gained notoriety for an alleged pattern of mysterious disappearances of ships and aircraft. These unexplained events have fueled numerous conspiracy theories, making the Bermuda Triangle one of the most enduring and enigmatic mysteries in popular culture.

The lore of the Bermuda Triangle gained significant attention in the mid-20th century, although reports of unusual incidents in the area date back much earlier. One of the earliest and most famous cases involves the disappearance of the USS Cyclops in 1918. The Cyclops, a massive naval ship, vanished without a trace along with its 309 crew members while en route from Barbados to Baltimore. No wreckage was ever found, leading to various conspiracy theories about what might have happened.

Another notable incident is the disappearance of Flight 19, a squadron of five U.S. Navy bombers that vanished during a training mission in December 1945. The planes, piloted by experienced airmen, lost radio contact and were never seen again. To add to the mystery, a search and rescue aircraft sent to find Flight 19 also disappeared, further fueling speculation and theories about the Bermuda Triangle.

Numerous other ships and planes have reportedly vanished under mysterious circumstances while traversing the Bermuda Triangle, each adding layers of intrigue to the legend. One significant case involves the SS Marine Sulphur Queen, a tanker that disappeared in 1963 with all 39 crew members. Another involves a commercial airliner that vanished in 1948 while flying from Puerto Rico to Miami.

One of the most pervasive conspiracy theories involves the idea that the Bermuda Triangle is a gateway or vortex to another dimension. Proponents of this theory suggest that ships and planes entering the area are transported to an alternate reality or parallel universe. This concept, while lacking empirical evidence, appeals to the imagination and has been a popular explanation in various books, documentaries, and films.

Another widely discussed theory posits that the Bermuda Triangle is a hotspot for extraterrestrial activity. According to this theory, UFOs are responsible for the disappearances, abducting ships and planes for unknown reasons. This idea gained traction with the publication of Charles Berlitz's "The Bermuda Triangle," which proposed that aliens might be studying human technology or using the Triangle as a base of operations. Despite the popularity of this theory in popular culture, there is no concrete evidence to support the existence of extraterrestrial involvement.

Some theories suggest that the Bermuda Triangle is home to advanced technology from a lost civilization, such as the mythical Atlantis. These theories propose that remnants of this advanced society, possibly located underwater, interfere with modern technology, causing ships and planes to vanish. The idea of Atlantis, popularized by the writings of Plato and subsequent authors, has been a rich source of speculation and fantasy.

Another conspiracy theory involves secret government experiments and military testing. Some theorists believe that the U.S. government, or other powerful entities, conduct clandestine operations in the Bermuda Triangle, leading to the disappearances. These theories often suggest that the area is used for testing advanced weapons, aircraft, or even time travel and teleportation technology. The lack of transparency and the presence of military bases in the region lend some credence to these speculations, although no definitive proof has been provided.

Magnetic anomalies are another commonly cited explanation for the Bermuda Triangle's mysteries. The area is known for irregularities in the Earth's magnetic field, which can cause compass malfunctions and navigational errors. Pilots and sailors have reported their compasses spinning erratically or pointing in the wrong direction while traversing the Triangle. Some conspiracy theorists suggest that these anomalies are the result of deliberate manipulation by secret organizations or unknown forces.

Human error and deliberate actions are also considered potential factors in the Bermuda Triangle's mysteries. Some theorists believe that navigational mistakes, equipment failures, or even acts of piracy could account for some of the disappearances. In some cases, ships and planes might have been deliberately scuttled or hijacked, leading to their unexplained vanishings. These more mundane explanations, while less sensational, are likely contributors to some of the incidents associated with the Bermuda Triangle.

One theory that has gained traction involves the influence of powerful oceanic currents and sudden underwater landslides. These natural phenomena could create dangerous conditions, such as massive waves or rapid changes in water density, leading to the sinking of ships and the crashing of aircraft. While this theory provides a plausible explanation for some of the disappearances, it does not account for all the incidents, particularly those involving aircraft.

The role of rogue waves has also been explored in relation to the Bermuda Triangle. These are extremely large and unexpected ocean waves that can pose significant dangers to even the largest vessels. While rogue waves are a recognized phenomenon, their occurrence in the Bermuda Triangle and their potential role in the region's mysteries are subjects of ongoing research and debate.

Despite the skepticism and scientific explanations, the Bermuda Triangle continues to fascinate and intrigue. Its mysteries have been explored in countless books, documentaries, and films, each offering different perspectives and theories. The enduring appeal of the Bermuda Triangle lies in its blend of science, myth, and adventure, providing fertile ground for the imagination.

The Bermuda Triangle's legacy extends beyond its geographical boundaries, symbolizing the human quest for understanding in the face of the unknown. It challenges our perceptions of reality and invites us to consider the limits of our knowledge. Whether viewed through the lens of science or fantasy, the Bermuda Triangle remains a powerful reminder of the mysteries that still exist in our world.

In recent years, advancements in technology and exploration have shed new light on some of the Bermuda Triangle's mysteries. Improved satellite imagery, underwater mapping, and forensic analysis have provided valuable tools for investigating the region's anomalies. While many questions remain unanswered, these technological advancements offer the potential for new discoveries and insights.

The Bermuda Triangle also serves as a case study in the power of narrative and the human tendency to seek patterns and explanations for unexplained phenomena. It highlights the interplay between fact and fiction, showing how stories can shape our understanding of the world. The enduring allure of the Bermuda Triangle lies in its ability to captivate the imagination and provoke curiosity, encouraging us to explore the boundaries of the unknown.

Chapter 7: The New World Order

The New World Order (NWO) is a conspiracy theory that suggests the existence of a secretive power elite with a globalist agenda conspiring to rule the world through an authoritarian one-world government. This theory posits that this shadowy cabal seeks to orchestrate various global events to manipulate economies, politics, and societies to achieve its goals of total world domination. The concept of the New World Order has been a focal point for many conspiracy theories, intertwining historical, political, and economic elements and reflecting fears of totalitarianism, loss of national sovereignty, and erosion of individual freedoms.

The idea of the New World Order is not a modern invention; it has roots in various historical contexts. One of the earliest references to a new world order can be traced back to the early 20th century. Following World War I, U.S. President Woodrow Wilson spoke of a new world order in terms of establishing international peace and cooperation, leading to the creation of the League of Nations. However, the modern conspiracy theory emerged more prominently during and after World War II, particularly with the establishment of the United Nations in 1945, which some saw as a step toward global governance.

The concept gained further traction during the Cold War, a period marked by intense geopolitical tensions and fears of nuclear annihilation. Both the Western and Eastern blocs were suspected of harboring ambitions for global control. The Bilderberg Group, founded in 1954, became a frequent target of conspiracy theorists. This annual conference, attended by influential business leaders, politicians, and intellectuals from North America and Europe, is viewed by some as a meeting of those planning the New World Order. Critics argue that the group's secrecy and elite membership fuel suspicions of a hidden agenda.

Another significant event that fueled New World Order conspiracy theories was the establishment of various international financial institutions, such as the International Monetary Fund (IMF) and the World Bank. These institutions, created to manage global economic stability, have been criticized for imposing policies that benefit wealthy nations at the expense of poorer ones, reinforcing the idea that a global elite manipulates economic systems for their gain.

In the 1990s, the term "New World Order" gained renewed attention after the fall of the Soviet Union and the end of the Cold War. U.S. President George H.W. Bush used the phrase in a 1990 speech to describe a world in which nations work together to achieve peace and security. This rhetoric, however, was interpreted by conspiracy theorists as evidence of a move towards a one-world government. The Gulf War and subsequent U.S. military interventions were seen as steps toward this goal.

The New World Order conspiracy theory encompasses a wide range of beliefs and interpretations. Some adherents focus on the role of international organizations and secret societies, such as the Trilateral Commission, the Council on Foreign Relations, and the Freemasons. These groups are believed to influence global politics and economics behind the scenes, often accused of manipulating events to create crises that justify the expansion of their control.

The theory also intersects with concerns about the erosion of national sovereignty. Proponents argue that globalist policies, such as trade agreements and supranational institutions like the European Union, undermine the autonomy of individual nations. The European Union, in particular, is often cited as a prototype of the New World Order, with its centralized governance and economic integration seen as steps toward a global government.

Economic globalization, characterized by the increased interdependence of national economies, is another focal point. Critics argue that globalization primarily benefits multinational corporations and the wealthy elite, leading to economic disparities and loss of local cultures and traditions. They contend that free trade agreements, deregulation, and privatization are tools used by the global elite to consolidate power and wealth.

The influence of the media is another critical aspect of the New World Order conspiracy theory. Mainstream media outlets are often accused of being complicit in the agenda, either through deliberate misinformation or by being controlled by corporate interests aligned with the New World Order. This belief has led to a distrust of traditional news sources and the rise of alternative media that claim to provide unfiltered, truthful information.

Technological advancements and surveillance are also seen as part of the New World Order's strategy. The increasing use of surveillance technologies, such as CCTV cameras, internet monitoring, and data collection by governments and corporations, is viewed as a means to control and monitor the population. The rise of social media and big data analytics has further intensified these fears, with concerns about privacy and the potential for misuse of personal information.

Health crises and pandemics are another area where the New World Order theory finds traction. Events like the 2009 H1N1 flu pandemic and the more recent COVID-19 pandemic have been interpreted by some as orchestrated efforts to impose draconian measures, such as lockdowns, mandatory vaccinations, and digital health passports, which are perceived as steps toward greater control over individuals.

The theory often incorporates elements of other conspiracies, such as those involving 9/11, climate change, and population control. For example, the 9/11 attacks are believed by some to have been a false flag operation designed to justify the invasion of Iraq and Afghanistan, expand military presence, and erode civil liberties through legislation like the USA PATRIOT Act. Similarly, climate change is viewed by some as a fabricated crisis intended to push for global environmental regulations and control over resources.

The idea of population control is also prevalent in New World Order theories. Some proponents believe that the global elite aim to reduce the world's population through means such as sterilization, engineered diseases, and promotion of contraceptives and abortion. These actions are perceived as attempts to maintain control over resources and ensure the dominance of a select few.

Religious and spiritual interpretations of the New World Order also exist. Some Christian fundamentalists view the New World Order as part of a prophetic End Times scenario, interpreting current events as fulfillment of biblical prophecies. They believe that a one-world government, led by the Antichrist, will emerge before the Second Coming of Christ. This perspective adds a layer of eschatological significance to the conspiracy theory.

Despite its wide-ranging and often contradictory elements, the New World Order conspiracy theory reflects deeper anxieties about power, control, and the direction of global affairs. It taps into fears of loss of autonomy, distrust of elites, and concerns about the impact of globalization and technological change. The theory's appeal lies in its ability to provide a comprehensive explanation for complex and often troubling global events, offering a sense of clarity and certainty in an increasingly interconnected and uncertain world.

The persistence of the New World Order theory is also facilitated by the internet and social media, which allow for the rapid dissemination of information and the formation of online communities. These platforms enable like-minded individuals to share ideas, reinforce beliefs, and challenge mainstream narratives. The echo chambers created by social media algorithms can amplify conspiracy theories, making them more resistant to counterarguments and evidence-based refutation.

Chapter 8: The Disappearance of Amelia Earhart

The disappearance of Amelia Earhart is one of the most enduring and intriguing mysteries of the 20th century. Earhart, an aviation pioneer and the first woman to fly solo across the Atlantic Ocean, vanished on July 2, 1937, during an attempt to circumnavigate the globe. Along with her navigator, Fred Noonan, Earhart was last heard from over the central Pacific Ocean near Howland Island. Despite extensive search efforts and countless investigations, no conclusive evidence has ever been found to determine their fate, leading to a myriad of theories and speculation.

Amelia Earhart was a trailblazer in the field of aviation. Born in 1897 in Atchison, Kansas, she developed a passion for flying at a young age. Earhart's achievements include being the first woman to fly solo across the Atlantic in 1932 and setting numerous altitude and speed records. By 1937, she had already achieved significant fame and was seen as a symbol of women's empowerment and adventure. Her attempt to fly around the world was meant to be the culmination of her illustrious career.

The round-the-world flight began on June 1, 1937, in Miami, Florida. Earhart and Noonan planned a westward route, flying through South America, Africa, the Indian subcontinent, and Southeast Asia. By late June, they had reached Lae, New Guinea, with about 7,000 miles left to cover over the Pacific Ocean. The next leg of their journey, from Lae to Howland Island, was the most challenging. Howland Island is a small, uninhabited coral island in the central Pacific, only about 1.5 miles long and half a mile wide, making it difficult to locate.

On July 2, 1937, Earhart and Noonan departed from Lae. They were equipped with radio communications, but the technology of the time was rudimentary compared to modern standards. Their last known position was near the Nukumanu Islands, about 800 miles into their 2,556-mile flight to Howland Island. At 7:42 AM, Earhart reported her position to the US Coast Guard cutter Itasca, stationed at Howland Island to assist with navigation. She indicated they were running low on fuel and struggling to locate the island. Her final transmission, at 8:43 AM, was garbled and unclear.

The disappearance triggered one of the largest search efforts in history. The United States Navy and Coast Guard scoured the ocean, covering an area of 250,000 square miles, but found no trace of Earhart, Noonan, or their plane. After two weeks, the official search was called off, though private searches continued for many years. The lack of evidence led to numerous theories about what might have happened.

One of the most widely accepted theories is that Earhart and Noonan simply ran out of fuel and crashed into the Pacific Ocean. This theory posits that they were unable to locate Howland Island due to navigational errors, radio communication issues, or adverse weather conditions. If they crashed into the ocean, the aircraft likely sank, making it difficult to find any wreckage. This explanation, while straightforward, leaves many questions unanswered and lacks definitive proof.

Another prominent theory suggests that Earhart and Noonan landed on Gardner Island (now Nikumaroro), part of the Phoenix Islands group, about 350 miles southeast of Howland Island. This hypothesis gained traction in 1940 when British colonial officer Gerald Gallagher discovered a partial human skeleton, a woman's shoe, and an improvised campsite on the island. Subsequent investigations by The International Group for Historic Aircraft Recovery (TIGHAR) have found artifacts and other evidence that some believe support this theory. However, no conclusive proof has been found, and the skeletal remains discovered in 1940 were lost, making definitive identification impossible.

A more controversial theory is that Earhart and Noonan were captured by the Japanese military. This theory posits that they veered off course and ended up in the Japanese-held Marshall Islands. According to this scenario, they were taken prisoner, and Earhart possibly died in captivity. Some variations of this theory suggest that Earhart was forced to become a Tokyo Rose broadcaster during World War II. Supporters of this theory cite anecdotal accounts and alleged sightings, but no credible evidence has ever emerged to substantiate these claims.

Another speculative theory involves a secret mission and spy work. Some believe that Earhart's flight was a cover for a government mission to gather intelligence on Japanese military activities in the Pacific. This theory suggests that her disappearance was orchestrated by the U.S. government, and she was either captured or went into hiding under a new identity. Like the Japanese capture theory, this idea lacks concrete evidence and is often regarded as more of a fanciful story than a plausible explanation.

The mystery of Amelia Earhart's disappearance has also inspired numerous searches for the wreckage of her aircraft. In recent years, advances in technology have renewed efforts to locate the plane. Deep-sea exploration teams have used sonar and underwater robots to search the ocean floor near Howland Island and other areas. While some searches have yielded intriguing findings, such as possible aircraft debris, none have definitively identified Earhart's Lockheed Electra.

Earhart's legacy extends beyond her disappearance. She remains an icon of aviation history and women's empowerment, celebrated for her daring spirit and pioneering achievements. The unsolved nature of her disappearance continues to captivate the public imagination, fueling endless speculation, books, documentaries, and films.

The fascination with Earhart's fate also reflects broader themes of exploration and adventure. Her story embodies the human desire to push boundaries and explore the unknown, even at great personal risk. The enduring mystery serves as a reminder of the challenges and uncertainties inherent in pioneering endeavors, particularly in the early days of aviation when technology and navigation were still developing.

In recent years, the search for answers has become more scientific and methodical. Organizations like TIGHAR have conducted multiple expeditions to Nikumaroro, employing archaeological techniques and forensic analysis to examine potential evidence. These efforts have yielded tantalizing clues, such as fragments of aircraft aluminum, a piece of glass that could be from a 1930s-style compact mirror, and bones that some researchers believe could be Earhart's. However, without definitive DNA evidence, the mystery remains unsolved.

The disappearance of Amelia Earhart also highlights the limitations of search and rescue operations in the vast expanse of the Pacific Ocean. Even with modern technology, locating a small aircraft or human remains in such a large and remote area is an immense challenge. The case underscores the need for continued advancements in search technology and international cooperation in search and rescue efforts.

Public interest in Earhart's story shows no signs of waning. Each new theory or piece of potential evidence reignites debate and speculation. The mystery has become a cultural touchstone, inspiring a wide range of interpretations and keeping Earhart's memory alive. Her life and career continue to inspire new generations of aviators and adventurers, reminding us of the enduring allure of flight and the quest for discovery.

Chapter 9: The Nazi Escape to Argentina

The Nazi escape to Argentina remains one of the most intriguing and debated episodes of post-World War II history. As the Third Reich crumbled in 1945, numerous high-ranking Nazi officials and collaborators sought refuge to avoid prosecution for war crimes. Argentina, under the presidency of Juan Domingo Perón, became one of the most notorious havens for these fugitives. Perón, who had pro-fascist sympathies and connections with European dictatorships, opened his country's doors to thousands of ex-Nazis, military officers, and collaborators. His motivations were multifaceted: ideological affinity, the desire to harness their skills and knowledge for Argentina's benefit, and the aspiration to build a stronger, more influential Argentina on the global stage.

The escape routes, often referred to as "ratlines," were complex networks that facilitated the movement of Nazis from Europe to South America. These routes were primarily orchestrated by a combination of former SS officers, sympathetic clergy within the Catholic Church, and various covert organizations. One of the most famous ratlines was operated by Bishop Alois Hudal, an Austrian cleric with strong Nazi ties, who used his position in the Vatican to provide travel documents and financial aid to fleeing Nazis. These escape routes typically began in Germany or Austria, leading through Italy, and then crossing the Atlantic to South America, with Argentina as a prime destination.

Once in Argentina, many Nazis were able to live relatively undisturbed lives, often under assumed identities. Some of the most infamous fugitives included Adolf Eichmann, Josef Mengele, and Erich Priebke. Eichmann, one of the architects of the Holocaust, managed to evade capture until 1960 when Israeli Mossad agents abducted him from his home in Buenos Aires and brought him to Israel to stand trial. Eichmann's capture and subsequent trial brought international attention to the issue of Nazi fugitives in Argentina and the broader South American continent.

Josef Mengele, the notorious doctor of Auschwitz known for his inhumane medical experiments on prisoners, managed to evade capture for decades. He lived in various South American countries, including Argentina, Paraguay, and Brazil, constantly moving to avoid detection. Mengele's death by drowning in Brazil in 1979 was only confirmed years later, leaving many questions about his life on the run.

Erich Priebke, a former SS officer involved in the massacre of 335 Italian civilians in the Ardeatine Caves, lived openly in Argentina under his own name for nearly 50 years. It wasn't until a 1994 American television interview exposed his presence that he was finally extradited to Italy, where he was tried and sentenced for his crimes.

The presence of Nazis in Argentina was an open secret, with various theories and rumors about the extent of their influence and the level of protection they received from the Argentine government. Some believe that the Perón government actively facilitated their escape and integration into Argentine society, providing them with new identities and employment opportunities. This alleged collaboration is seen as part of Perón's broader strategy to leverage the expertise of former Nazis to bolster Argentina's scientific, military, and intelligence capabilities.

The Argentine government's involvement in harboring Nazis was part of a larger pattern of post-war geopolitical maneuvering. During the Cold War, both the United States and the Soviet Union were keen to recruit former Nazis for their own purposes, particularly in the fields of rocketry, intelligence, and military strategy. Operation Paperclip, the U.S. program that brought German scientists to America, including Wernher von Braun, is a well-documented example of this pragmatic, if morally ambiguous, approach.

In Argentina, the Nazis found a relatively hospitable environment. The country had a sizable German community, and there were established networks that could provide support and cover for the fugitives. Additionally, the Perón government, eager to modernize the nation, saw the influx of skilled individuals—regardless of their past—as an opportunity to advance Argentina's technological and scientific development.

The legacy of the Nazi escape to Argentina has been the subject of numerous investigations, books, and films. The precise number of Nazis who fled to Argentina remains uncertain, with estimates ranging from a few hundred to several thousand. This uncertainty is compounded by the clandestine nature of their escape and the lack of comprehensive records. Nevertheless, the presence of high-profile war criminals like Eichmann and Mengele underscores the significant role Argentina played as a sanctuary for those fleeing justice.

The story of the Nazi escape to Argentina continues to capture the public imagination, reflecting broader themes of justice, accountability, and the complexities of post-war geopolitics. It raises important questions about the complicity of governments and institutions in aiding war criminals and the lengths to which individuals will go to evade responsibility for their actions. The narratives of those who escaped, those who pursued them, and the countries that harbored them are intertwined in a complex web that highlights the enduring impact of World War II on global history and memory.

Chapter 10: The Black Dahlia Murder

The Black Dahlia murder, one of the most infamous unsolved crimes in American history, occurred in Los Angeles in 1947. Elizabeth Short, a 22-year-old aspiring actress, was brutally murdered and her body was discovered on January 15, 1947, in a vacant lot in the Leimert Park neighborhood. The severity and grotesque nature of the crime, combined with the media frenzy that followed, cemented the case in the annals of criminal lore.

Elizabeth Short, born on July 29, 1924, in Boston, Massachusetts, had moved to California in pursuit of a Hollywood career. She was often depicted as a young woman with dreams of stardom, though she faced numerous struggles, including financial instability and transient living conditions. Short's striking appearance and penchant for wearing black clothing earned her the nickname "The Black Dahlia," a moniker that was sensationalized by the press.

On the morning of January 15, 1947, a mother and her young child discovered Short's mutilated body. The scene was horrifying: her body had been severed at the waist, and she had been posed with her arms raised above her head and her legs spread apart. The body was drained of blood, and there were extensive lacerations on her face, including a Glasgow smile—slashes extending from the corners of her mouth to her ears. These gruesome details immediately captured the attention of the media and the public.

The Los Angeles Police Department launched an extensive investigation, with hundreds of officers and detectives assigned to the case. The autopsy revealed that Short had been dead for about ten hours before her body was discovered. She had suffered severe trauma before death, including blows to the head, and it was determined that she had been tortured for several hours before being killed. The cause of death was ruled as hemorrhage and shock from the blows to the head and the cutting of her body.

The media frenzy surrounding the case was unprecedented. Newspapers and radio stations provided sensationalized coverage, often focusing on Short's personal life and portraying her in a lurid light. This sensationalism not only captivated the public but also complicated the investigation by generating a deluge of false leads and confessions. Over the years, more than 50 people confessed to the murder, but none of these confessions were credible, and the case remained unsolved.

The investigation into the Black Dahlia murder was marked by numerous theories and suspects. One of the most prominent suspects was George Hodel, a wealthy Los Angeles doctor. Hodel came under suspicion due to his alleged connections to the victim and his questionable behavior. In the early 2000s, Hodel's son, Steve Hodel, a retired LAPD detective, published a book implicating his father in the murder. Steve Hodel presented circumstantial evidence, including diary entries, photographs, and Hodel's proximity to the crime scene, but definitive proof has remained elusive.

Another theory posits that the Black Dahlia murder was the work of an unknown serial killer. Some investigators and researchers have suggested that Short's murder bore similarities to other unsolved homicides in the Los Angeles area during the same period, leading to speculation that a single individual might have been responsible for multiple killings. However, no concrete evidence has been found to support this theory.

The Black Dahlia case also spawned numerous conspiracy theories, ranging from involvement by corrupt police officials to connections with Hollywood elites and organized crime. Some theorists have suggested that the murder was covered up or mishandled by authorities due to the involvement of influential individuals. These theories, while intriguing, have not been substantiated by credible evidence.

In the decades since the murder, the Black Dahlia case has remained a subject of intense fascination and speculation. It has inspired countless books, films, and television shows, each offering its own interpretation of the events and possible solutions to the mystery. The case's enduring allure lies in its combination of a gruesome crime, a beautiful and enigmatic victim, and a web of tantalizing clues that have never quite come together to form a complete picture.

The impact of the Black Dahlia murder extends beyond the realm of true crime. It has influenced popular culture, shaping the noir aesthetic that became synonymous with post-war Los Angeles. The case has also prompted discussions about the treatment of women in the media and the ways in which victims of violent crimes are often sensationalized and objectified. Elizabeth Short's life and death have been the subject of numerous works of fiction and non-fiction, each contributing to the ongoing mythos surrounding the case.

Despite the passage of time, the Black Dahlia murder remains one of the most captivating and mysterious unsolved crimes in American history. Advances in forensic science and investigative techniques have occasionally renewed hopes that the case might one day be solved, but so far, the identity of Elizabeth Short's killer remains unknown. The Black Dahlia murder stands as a haunting reminder of the dark underbelly of Hollywood's golden age and the enduring quest for justice in the face of seemingly insurmountable odds.

Chapter 11: The Death of Princess Diana

The death of Princess Diana, a tragic event that shook the world, occurred on August 31, 1997. Diana, Princess of Wales, died as a result of injuries sustained in a car crash in the Pont de l'Alma tunnel in Paris, France. Her companion, Dodi Fayed, and the driver, Henri Paul, also perished in the crash. The only survivor was Diana's bodyguard, Trevor Rees-Jones, who suffered severe injuries. The death of Princess Diana, often referred to as the "People's Princess," sparked a global outpouring of grief and led to numerous conspiracy theories regarding the circumstances surrounding the accident.

Princess Diana was born Diana Frances Spencer on July 1, 1961, into an aristocratic British family. She married Charles, Prince of Wales, in 1981, in a ceremony watched by millions around the world. Diana quickly became a beloved figure, admired for her beauty, compassion, and charitable work. She was particularly known for her efforts to raise awareness about HIV/AIDS, leprosy, and the dangers of landmines. Her marriage to Prince Charles, however, was fraught with difficulties, and the couple divorced in 1996 after years of public and private turmoil.

In the summer of 1997, Diana began a relationship with Dodi Fayed, the son of Egyptian billionaire Mohamed Al-Fayed. On the night of August 30, 1997, Diana and Dodi were staying at the Ritz Hotel in Paris, owned by Mohamed Al-Fayed. They decided to leave the hotel shortly after midnight, intending to return to Dodi's apartment. To evade paparazzi, they left from the hotel's rear entrance and entered a Mercedes-Benz S280 driven by Henri Paul, the Ritz's deputy head of security. Trevor Rees-Jones was in the front passenger seat, with Diana and Dodi in the back.

As the car sped away, it was pursued by photographers on motorcycles. At approximately 12:23 AM, the vehicle entered the Pont de l'Alma tunnel. Traveling at high speed, Henri Paul lost control of the car, which collided with a pillar in the tunnel. The impact was catastrophic. Dodi Fayed and Henri Paul were pronounced dead at the scene, while Diana was critically injured. Emergency services arrived quickly, and Diana was taken to the Pitié-Salpêtrière Hospital. Despite efforts to save her, she succumbed to her injuries at around 4:00 AM.

The immediate aftermath of the crash was marked by shock and disbelief. The news of Diana's death spread rapidly, and tributes poured in from around the world. In the United Kingdom, the public reaction was one of profound grief, with thousands of mourners leaving flowers, messages, and memorabilia outside Kensington Palace, Diana's London residence. The British royal family, staying at Balmoral Castle in Scotland at the time, faced criticism for their perceived delay in addressing the public's grief. Queen Elizabeth II later made a televised address, expressing her admiration for Diana and sharing in the nation's sorrow.

The official investigation into the crash, conducted by French authorities, concluded that Henri Paul was responsible for the accident due to his reckless driving and intoxication. Toxicology reports revealed that Paul had a blood alcohol level over three times the legal limit in France and had traces of prescription drugs in his system. The paparazzi chasing the car were also scrutinized, with many blaming their aggressive pursuit for contributing to the crash. Several photographers were initially charged with manslaughter but were later cleared.

Despite the official findings, numerous conspiracy theories emerged, suggesting that Diana's death was not an accident but rather the result of a deliberate plot. Mohamed Al-Fayed was one of the most vocal proponents of these theories, alleging that the British establishment, including the royal family and intelligence services, orchestrated the crash to prevent Diana from marrying Dodi and potentially having a child with him. Al-Fayed claimed that such a union would be unacceptable to the British monarchy and feared that Diana might reveal damaging secrets about the royal family.

These conspiracy theories gained traction in part due to several unresolved questions and inconsistencies. Some pointed to the role of the paparazzi, who were known to hound Diana relentlessly, while others questioned the actions and background of Henri Paul, who was discovered to have significant sums of money in his bank accounts, leading to speculation about whether he might have been bribed or coerced. Additionally, there were claims about a mysterious white Fiat Uno seen near the crash site and allegations that Diana had expressed fears for her safety in letters to friends.

In 2004, the British government launched an inquest into Diana's death, led by Lord Justice Scott Baker. The inquest examined extensive evidence, including eyewitness testimonies, forensic reports, and expert analysis. In 2008, the jury concluded that Diana and Dodi were unlawfully killed due to the grossly negligent driving of Henri Paul and the pursuing paparazzi. The jury's verdict dismissed the conspiracy theories, affirming that the crash was a tragic accident.

Despite the official conclusions, the death of Princess Diana continues to be the subject of intense fascination and speculation. Her legacy endures not only through her charitable work but also through her sons, Prince William and Prince Harry, who have both spoken publicly about their mother's influence on their lives and their ongoing efforts to honor her memory. Diana's death also had a lasting impact on the British royal family and their relationship with the media and the public. The outpouring of grief and the subsequent criticism of the monarchy led to significant changes in how the royal family engages with the public and addresses issues of mental health and personal privacy.

Princess Diana's life and tragic death have been commemorated in numerous books, documentaries, and films, each exploring different aspects of her legacy and the enduring mystery surrounding the events of August 31, 1997. The fascination with her story reflects broader themes of celebrity, media scrutiny, and the human cost of fame. As the world continues to remember Diana, the People's Princess, her legacy of compassion, kindness, and advocacy for the vulnerable remains a beacon of hope and inspiration.

Chapter 12: The UFO Sighting at Area 51

The UFO sighting at Area 51 is one of the most enduring and fascinating topics within the realm of extraterrestrial theories and government conspiracy discussions. Area 51, officially known as Groom Lake or Homey Airport, is a highly classified United States Air Force facility located within the Nevada Test and Training Range. The site has been the subject of numerous rumors and speculations, particularly concerning its alleged involvement with UFOs and extraterrestrial technology.

The origins of Area 51 as a center of mystery and intrigue date back to the Cold War era. Established in the 1950s, the facility was initially used for testing and developing advanced military aircraft. One of the most notable projects associated with Area 51 was the development of the U-2 reconnaissance aircraft, which began in 1955. The isolated location, with its vast desert landscape and restricted airspace, made it an ideal site for testing secretive projects away from prying eyes.

The connection between Area 51 and UFO sightings gained significant traction in the late 1980s, largely due to the claims of a man named Bob Lazar. In 1989, Lazar gave an interview to a Las Vegas television station, KLAS-TV, in which he claimed to have worked as a physicist at a site called S-4 near Area 51. According to Lazar, his job involved reverse-engineering extraterrestrial technology recovered from crashed alien spacecraft. He described in detail several flying saucers that he alleged were stored at the facility, claiming that they utilized a form of propulsion based on an element he referred to as "Element 115," which allowed the craft to manipulate gravity.

Lazar's claims were met with a mix of skepticism and intrigue. While many dismissed his story as a hoax or fabrication, it resonated with a public already captivated by the idea of extraterrestrial life and government cover-ups. His allegations sparked a renewed interest in Area 51, leading to an explosion of speculation and conspiracy theories. Supporters of Lazar's claims pointed to the secrecy surrounding Area 51 as evidence that the government was hiding something extraordinary.

In the decades following Lazar's revelations, Area 51 became synonymous with UFOs and extraterrestrial activity. The site attracted the attention of researchers, enthusiasts, and media outlets worldwide. Numerous books, documentaries, and television shows explored the mysteries of Area 51, often presenting it as the epicenter of a vast government conspiracy to conceal the truth about alien visitors and advanced technology.

One of the most famous UFO sightings associated with Area 51 occurred on July 7, 1947, in Roswell, New Mexico, predating the site's establishment but becoming inextricably linked with it in popular culture. The Roswell Incident involved the recovery of debris from what the U.S. military initially described as a "flying disc" but later claimed was a weather balloon. The conflicting reports and subsequent secrecy fueled widespread speculation that the debris was from an extraterrestrial spacecraft and that alien bodies had been recovered and transported to Area 51 for study.

The U.S. government's handling of UFO sightings and reports added to the aura of mystery surrounding Area 51. In 1952, the U.S. Air Force launched Project Blue Book, a systematic study of UFOs and their potential threat to national security. While the project concluded in 1969, stating that most UFO sightings could be explained by natural phenomena or man-made objects, it did little to quell public fascination or belief in government cover-ups. The declassification of documents related to Project Blue Book in the 1970s and 1980s revealed that a small percentage of sightings remained unexplained, further fueling speculation.

In the 1990s, the Freedom of Information Act led to the release of more documents about Area 51, including its role in the development of advanced aircraft such as the U-2, A-12, and SR-71 Blackbird. These revelations provided some context for the secrecy surrounding the site, explaining that many UFO sightings in the vicinity were likely the result of classified aircraft tests. However, for many enthusiasts, this information only scratched the surface of the mysteries they believed were being concealed.

In 2013, the CIA officially acknowledged the existence of Area 51 for the first time, releasing documents detailing its history and the projects conducted there. The admission confirmed what had long been suspected: that Area 51 was a hub for testing experimental aircraft and weapons systems. Despite this acknowledgment, the specifics of many projects remained classified, and the government provided no information about extraterrestrial technology or alien life forms, leaving room for continued speculation.

The cultural impact of Area 51 and its association with UFOs is significant. The site has inspired countless works of fiction, from films and television shows to books and video games. Iconic movies like "Independence Day" and "Close Encounters of the Third Kind" have incorporated themes of government secrecy and alien encounters, often featuring Area 51 as a central element. These cultural representations have both reflected and reinforced public fascination with the idea that the government is hiding the truth about extraterrestrial visitors.

The lore surrounding Area 51 reached a new height of public engagement in 2019, when a Facebook event titled "Storm Area 51, They Can't Stop All of Us" went viral. The event, initially intended as a joke, proposed that large numbers of people gather to storm the highly secure facility in search of evidence of aliens. The idea captured the imagination of millions, leading to widespread media coverage and prompting both the U.S. Air Force and local authorities to issue warnings about the dangers of attempting to breach the site. Although the event itself saw only a modest turnout, it underscored the enduring fascination with Area 51 and the widespread belief that it harbors extraordinary secrets.

Despite the lack of concrete evidence proving the existence of extraterrestrial technology at Area 51, the site's reputation as a focal point for UFO lore and conspiracy theories persists. This enduring intrigue is fueled by the combination of government secrecy, credible eyewitness accounts of unexplained phenomena, and the human desire to believe in something beyond our current understanding of the universe. The UFO sightings at Area 51 continue to captivate the public imagination, embodying the tension between skepticism and belief, science and speculation, and the known and the unknown.

The continued interest in Area 51 and UFO sightings has also spurred scientific inquiry and public advocacy for greater transparency. Organizations like the Mutual UFO Network (MUFON) and the Center for the Study of Extraterrestrial Intelligence (CSETI) work to investigate and document UFO sightings, advocating for the disclosure of government-held information. Additionally, recent developments, such as the release of U.S. Navy videos showing unidentified aerial phenomena and the establishment of the Pentagon's Unidentified Aerial Phenomena Task Force, indicate a growing willingness among government and military officials to address and investigate unexplained aerial encounters.

Chapter 13: The Philadelphia Experiment

The Philadelphia Experiment is one of the most intriguing and controversial urban legends in the realm of government conspiracies and paranormal phenomena. It centers on the alleged secret U.S. Navy project, codenamed "Project Rainbow," which supposedly took place in October 1943 at the Philadelphia Naval Shipyard. The objective of the experiment was to render the USS Eldridge (DE-173), a Cannon-class destroyer escort, invisible to radar and possibly to the naked eye. The story combines elements of advanced technology, wartime secrecy, and alleged cover-ups, making it a captivating subject for conspiracy theorists and enthusiasts of the unexplained.

The origins of the Philadelphia Experiment legend trace back to the 1950s, largely due to the claims made by a man named Carl M. Allen, who later became known by the pseudonym Carlos Miguel Allende. Allen claimed to have witnessed the experiment while serving aboard the SS Andrew Furuseth, a merchant ship docked in the Philadelphia Naval Shipyard at the time. In 1955, he sent a series of letters to Morris K. Jessup, an astronomer and UFO enthusiast, detailing the supposed events of the experiment. Jessup had authored a book called "The Case for the UFO," which discussed unidentified flying objects and advanced propulsion theories, attracting Allen's attention.

According to Allen, the USS Eldridge was fitted with specialized equipment, including powerful generators and electromagnetic field devices, in an effort to achieve radar invisibility. He claimed that the experiment went far beyond its intended scope, allegedly causing the ship to become not only invisible but also to teleport from Philadelphia to Norfolk, Virginia, and back again within a matter of minutes. Furthermore, Allen described horrifying side effects experienced by the crew, including severe disorientation, mental instability, and even physical afflictions. Some sailors were purportedly fused with the metal structures of the ship, while others vanished entirely or were driven insane.

The Philadelphia Experiment narrative gained further attention when Jessup received an annotated copy of his book, filled with comments and notes in three different handwriting styles, supposedly from Allen and two other individuals. These annotations elaborated on the experiment and hinted at a vast cover-up involving the U.S. Navy and extraterrestrial technology. The annotated book was eventually brought to the attention of the Office of Naval Research (ONR), which conducted a brief inquiry but ultimately dismissed the claims as unfounded.

Despite the lack of official confirmation, the Philadelphia Experiment legend persisted, fueled by a combination of public fascination and speculation. Over the years, numerous authors, researchers, and filmmakers have explored and expanded upon the story, each adding their own interpretations and embellishments. Some versions suggest that the experiment was part of a broader effort to develop advanced stealth technology and teleportation capabilities, potentially involving collaboration with alien beings or the use of exotic matter.

In the 1970s and 1980s, the Philadelphia Experiment resurfaced in popular culture, thanks in part to the work of authors such as Charles Berlitz and William L. Moore, who published a book titled "The Philadelphia Experiment: Project Invisibility" in 1979. Berlitz and Moore's book drew heavily on Allen's original claims and incorporated additional testimony from alleged witnesses and experts. They posited that the experiment was a real, albeit highly classified, military operation that went disastrously wrong. The book's release reignited public interest and inspired a 1984 science fiction film, "The

Philadelphia Experiment," which dramatized the events and introduced the story to a new generation.

Skeptics and debunkers, however, have raised significant doubts about the veracity of the Philadelphia Experiment claims. Critics point to inconsistencies in the timeline, the lack of corroborating evidence, and the implausibility of the described phenomena from a scientific standpoint. The USS Eldridge's logbooks and wartime records, for instance, indicate that the ship was never in Philadelphia during the purported time of the experiment. Additionally, the supposed eyewitnesses and their accounts have been scrutinized, with many discrepancies and contradictions emerging over the years.

One explanation offered by skeptics is that the Philadelphia Experiment legend may have originated from a combination of wartime misinformation, misunderstandings, and the imagination of individuals like Carl Allen. During World War II, the U.S. Navy was indeed conducting experiments related to degaussing, a technique used to reduce the magnetic signatures of ships to protect them from magnetic mines and torpedoes. Some theorists suggest that these degaussing experiments, which involved wrapping ships in electrical cables and generating electromagnetic fields, might have been misinterpreted or exaggerated into the Philadelphia Experiment story.

Another factor that may have contributed to the legend is the concept of "invisibility" in a more metaphorical sense. In the context of wartime secrecy and intelligence operations, the notion of rendering a ship "invisible" could have referred to making it undetectable by enemy radar or observers, rather than literal physical invisibility or teleportation. This more plausible interpretation aligns with known military technologies and objectives of the time, though it lacks the sensational and supernatural elements that have captivated the public imagination.

Despite these rational explanations, the Philadelphia Experiment continues to be a subject of fascination and debate. Its enduring appeal lies in the blending of historical context, technological speculation, and paranormal intrigue. The story touches on deep-seated themes of government secrecy, the pursuit of forbidden knowledge, and the potential consequences of tampering with the fundamental forces of nature.

In recent years, the Philadelphia Experiment has also intersected with other conspiracy theories and fringe science concepts, such as time travel, alternate dimensions, and the Montauk Project—a supposed continuation of the Philadelphia Experiment involving mind control and temporal manipulation. These connections have further expanded the mythos, creating a complex web of narratives that defy easy resolution.

The Philadelphia Experiment serves as a case study in how legends and conspiracies can evolve and persist in the collective consciousness. It highlights the power of storytelling, the allure of the unknown, and the human tendency to seek patterns and meaning in the face of uncertainty. Whether viewed as a cautionary tale, a historical curiosity, or a genuine mystery, the Philadelphia Experiment remains an enduring and provocative topic that continues to inspire curiosity and speculation.

Chapter 14: The Jonestown Massacre

The Jonestown Massacre, also known as the Jonestown tragedy, is one of the most harrowing and infamous events in modern history. It took place on November 18, 1978, in the remote jungle settlement of Jonestown in Guyana, South America. The massacre resulted in the deaths of 918 people, most of whom were members of the Peoples Temple, a cult led by Reverend Jim Jones. The event stands as a stark reminder of the dangers of unchecked charismatic leadership, cult dynamics, and the tragic consequences of blind obedience and manipulation.

The origins of the Peoples Temple trace back to the 1950s, when Jim Jones, a charismatic preacher with a vision of a racially integrated and utopian society, founded the church in Indianapolis, Indiana. Jones' early ministry was marked by a commitment to social justice, civil rights, and helping the poor and disenfranchised. He adopted children of different racial backgrounds, calling them his "Rainbow Family," and attracted a diverse following of individuals who were drawn to his message of equality and communal living.

In the 1960s, Jones moved the Peoples Temple to California, establishing congregations in Ukiah, San Francisco, and Los Angeles. The church continued to grow, and Jones became increasingly influential in political and social circles. He was known for his charismatic oratory, faith healing demonstrations, and the church's extensive social programs, which included free medical clinics, legal aid, and community outreach. However, beneath the surface, Jones' leadership began to exhibit signs of authoritarianism, paranoia, and manipulation.

By the early 1970s, reports of abuse, financial mismanagement, and coercive practices within the Peoples Temple began to surface. Former members and concerned relatives raised allegations of physical punishment, forced labor, and psychological manipulation. These allegations drew the attention of the media and law enforcement, increasing scrutiny on Jones and his organization. In response, Jones sought to distance the church from the growing criticism and embarked on a new venture that would ultimately lead to tragedy.

In 1974, Jones leased land in Guyana, a small South American country, with the intention of establishing a self-sufficient agricultural commune where his followers could live free from persecution. He named the settlement "Jonestown" and began relocating members of the Peoples Temple to the remote jungle outpost. By 1977, approximately 1,000 members had moved to Jonestown, lured by promises of a utopian society and Jones' assurances of safety and security.

Life in Jonestown was harsh and controlled. The settlement was isolated, with limited communication with the outside world. Residents worked long hours in the fields and endured strict rules and surveillance. Jones' behavior became increasingly erratic; he used loudspeakers to broadcast his sermons and speeches day and night, instilling a sense of paranoia and fear among the inhabitants. He spoke of imminent threats from the outside world, particularly from the U.S. government and defectors, reinforcing the idea that Jonestown was a sanctuary from a hostile and corrupt society.

As conditions in Jonestown deteriorated, concerned relatives and former members in the United States intensified their efforts to expose the abuses within the Peoples Temple. This led to the involvement of Congressman Leo Ryan, a U.S. representative from California, who decided to personally investigate the situation in Jonestown. In November 1978, Ryan, accompanied by a delegation of journalists, relatives of temple members, and concerned citizens, traveled to Guyana to assess the conditions and speak with residents.

Ryan's visit initially seemed to go well, with Jones and his followers putting on a facade of normalcy and contentment. However, behind the scenes, tensions were high. Some residents saw Ryan's visit as an opportunity to escape Jonestown and sought his help in leaving. On November 18, during a visit to the nearby Port Kaituma airstrip, several residents attempted to flee with Ryan's delegation. This act of defection triggered a violent response from Jones and his loyalists.

As Ryan and his group prepared to board planes to leave, they were ambushed by armed members of the Peoples Temple security force. In the ensuing attack, Congressman Ryan, three journalists, and a defector were killed, while several others were wounded. The remaining delegation members managed to escape, but the violence at the airstrip marked the beginning of the end for Jonestown.

Back at the settlement, Jones ordered his followers to gather in the central pavilion. In a chilling and coercive speech, he declared that the community was under attack and that their only option was to commit "revolutionary suicide." He presented this as an act of defiance against oppression and a means of maintaining their dignity. Bowls of a cyanide-laced drink, often referred to as "Flavor Aid" (though commonly mistaken for Kool-Aid), were prepared, and parents were instructed to administer the poison to their children before taking it themselves.

The atmosphere in the pavilion was a mixture of fear, confusion, and resignation. Some members willingly followed Jones' orders, while others protested or tried to escape. Armed guards ensured compliance, and those who resisted were forcibly injected with the poison. In a matter of minutes, hundreds of people, including children, infants, and the elderly, lay dead or dying. The sight of the mass suicide was horrifying, with bodies strewn across the pavilion and surrounding areas.

By the time authorities arrived, the scene was one of utter devastation. A total of 918 people perished in Jonestown, including 304 children. The tragedy was one of the largest mass suicides in modern history and left an indelible mark on the collective consciousness. The aftermath of the Jonestown Massacre sparked widespread outrage, sorrow, and disbelief. It prompted extensive media coverage, government investigations, and a reevaluation of the dangers posed by cults and extremist movements.

The legacy of Jonestown is multifaceted, encompassing themes of charismatic leadership, manipulation, and the psychological dynamics of cults. Jim Jones' ability to command absolute loyalty from his followers, despite his increasingly erratic and abusive behavior, highlights the powerful influence of charismatic authority. His rhetoric of social justice and utopian ideals, coupled with fear-mongering and isolation, created an environment where critical thinking was suppressed, and obedience was enforced through psychological and physical coercion.

The Jonestown tragedy also underscored the vulnerabilities of individuals seeking belonging and purpose. Many Peoples Temple members were drawn to the church by its promises of equality, community, and social change. They were often marginalized individuals who found solace and meaning in Jones' vision. This sense of belonging and purpose, however, was exploited by Jones, who manipulated their trust and loyalty to serve his own ends.

In the years following the massacre, survivors and family members of the victims have sought to understand and come to terms with the events of Jonestown. Many have shared their stories and experiences, providing valuable insights into the dynamics of the Peoples Temple and the psychological mechanisms that allowed such a tragedy to occur. Their testimonies contribute to a broader understanding of the dangers posed by cults and the importance of vigilance in recognizing and addressing signs of manipulation and abuse.

The Jonestown Massacre remains a poignant reminder of the potential for human vulnerability to be exploited by charismatic leaders and extremist ideologies. It serves as a cautionary tale about the perils of blind obedience, the power of manipulation, and the devastating consequences that can arise when individuals surrender their autonomy and critical thinking. The tragedy of Jonestown continues to resonate as a stark warning about the importance of safeguarding individual freedom, promoting mental health awareness, and fostering environments where people can seek meaning and community without falling prey to exploitation and abuse.

Chapter 15: The CIA's MK-Ultra Program

The CIA's MK-Ultra program, also known as Project MK-Ultra, was a covert operation launched by the Central Intelligence Agency (CIA) in the 1950s and continued through the 1960s. The program aimed to explore and develop methods of mind control, interrogation techniques, and chemical manipulation of the human psyche. It has since become one of the most infamous and controversial programs in the history of U.S. intelligence, symbolizing the ethical and moral boundaries that can be crossed in the name of national security and scientific advancement.

The origins of MK-Ultra can be traced back to the early Cold War era, a time of intense geopolitical tension and competition between the United States and the Soviet Union. In the wake of World War II, reports emerged of Soviet, Chinese, and North Korean forces using mind control techniques on prisoners of war and political detainees. These reports alarmed U.S. intelligence agencies and spurred a race to understand and develop countermeasures against potential threats. The CIA, under the leadership of Director Allen Dulles, initiated MK-Ultra as part of this effort.

Officially sanctioned on April 13, 1953, MK-Ultra was directed by Sidney Gottlieb, a chemist and CIA officer. The program's scope was vast, encompassing a wide range of experiments and research initiatives. These included the study of drugs, hypnosis, sensory deprivation, isolation, verbal and sexual abuse, and other forms of psychological manipulation. The overarching goal was to discover techniques that could be used to control or alter human behavior, enhance interrogation methods, and potentially develop "truth serums" or other mind-altering substances that could be used in espionage and covert operations.

One of the most well-known and controversial aspects of MK-Ultra was its experimentation with LSD (lysergic acid diethylamide). LSD was first synthesized by Swiss chemist Albert Hofmann in 1938, but its powerful psychoactive effects were not discovered until 1943. The CIA became interested in the drug's potential for altering perception, cognition, and behavior. Under MK-Ultra, the agency conducted extensive experiments with LSD, administering the drug to both willing and unwitting subjects to observe its effects.

These experiments took place in various settings, including hospitals, prisons, universities, and CIA safe houses. In many cases, subjects were not informed about the true nature of the experiments or the substances they were being given. One notorious instance involved the unwitting administration of LSD to CIA officer Frank Olson, who experienced a severe psychological crisis and ultimately fell to his death from a hotel window in 1953. Olson's death was initially ruled a suicide, but later investigations suggested that he may have been murdered to cover up the experiments.

In addition to LSD, MK-Ultra researchers experimented with other drugs, such as mescaline, psilocybin, and various barbiturates and amphetamines. These substances were tested for their potential to induce confessions, enhance suggestibility, and manipulate memory. Subjects were often subjected to extreme and unethical treatment, including prolonged periods of sensory deprivation, isolation, and forced drug administration. The ethical violations and lack of informed consent in these experiments have been widely criticized and condemned.

MK-Ultra also explored the use of hypnosis and other psychological techniques. The program aimed to investigate whether hypnosis could be used to create "Manchurian candidates" – individuals who could be programmed to carry out actions against their will or without their conscious awareness. These experiments sought to determine if subjects could be hypnotically induced to commit acts of espionage, sabotage, or assassination. While there is no conclusive evidence that MK-Ultra succeeded in creating such candidates, the very pursuit of these goals raises significant ethical and moral questions.

The reach of MK-Ultra extended beyond the United States, as the CIA collaborated with institutions and researchers in Canada and Europe. One of the most infamous international collaborations involved Dr. Ewen Cameron, a Scottish-born psychiatrist who conducted MK-Ultra-funded experiments at the Allan Memorial Institute in Montreal, Canada. Cameron's experiments, which he called "psychic driving," involved intensive and often brutal methods, including drug-induced comas, high-dose electroconvulsive therapy, and repetitive audio messages aimed at breaking down and reprogramming patients' minds. Many of Cameron's subjects suffered long-term psychological damage as a result of these experiments.

The secrecy surrounding MK-Ultra began to unravel in the early 1970s, following the Watergate scandal and increasing public scrutiny of government activities. In 1974, investigative journalist Seymour Hersh published an article in The New York Times exposing the CIA's domestic surveillance and covert operations, including MK-Ultra. This revelation prompted a series of government investigations, most notably the Church Committee, chaired by Senator Frank Church, and the Rockefeller Commission, led by Vice President Nelson Rockefeller. These investigations uncovered extensive documentation of MK-Ultra and its various subprojects, revealing the breadth and ethical violations of the program.

In 1977, during Senate hearings on MK-Ultra, CIA Director Stansfield Turner admitted that the agency had conducted mind control experiments and apologized for the program's abuses. However, much of the documentation related to MK-Ultra had been destroyed on the orders of former CIA Director Richard Helms in 1973, making it difficult to fully assess the scope and impact of the program. Despite the destruction of records, enough evidence remained to paint a disturbing picture of a program that operated with little oversight and accountability.

The legacy of MK-Ultra has had a lasting impact on public perception of the CIA and government operations. It has contributed to a deep-seated mistrust of intelligence agencies and fueled numerous conspiracy theories. The ethical breaches and human rights violations committed under the program have been widely condemned by historians, ethicists, and the public. The revelations of MK-Ultra have also prompted calls for greater transparency, oversight, and accountability in government research and intelligence activities.

In the years following the exposure of MK-Ultra, efforts have been made to provide restitution and support to the victims of the program. Several lawsuits have been filed against the CIA and associated institutions, resulting in financial settlements and public apologies. The Canadian government, for instance, reached settlements with former patients of Dr. Ewen Cameron's experiments, acknowledging the harm caused and providing compensation.

MK-Ultra has also influenced popular culture, inspiring numerous books, films, and television shows that explore themes of mind control, government conspiracies, and the ethical boundaries of scientific research. Works such as the film "The Manchurian Candidate," the television series "The X-Files," and the novel "Firestarter" by Stephen King have drawn on the themes and controversies of MK-Ultra, reflecting the program's enduring impact on the collective imagination.

In addition to its cultural influence, MK-Ultra has raised important ethical and philosophical questions about the limits of scientific inquiry and the responsibilities of researchers and government agencies. The program serves as a cautionary tale about the potential for scientific advancements to be misused and the importance of ethical guidelines and oversight in research. It underscores the need for informed consent, respect for human dignity, and the protection of individual rights in all scientific and medical endeavors.

The story of MK-Ultra is a complex and disturbing chapter in the history of U.S. intelligence and scientific research. It reveals the dark side of the quest for knowledge and the potential for ethical transgressions in the pursuit of national security and scientific advancement. As such, it remains a powerful reminder of the importance of ethical principles, transparency, and accountability in all areas of research and government activity.

Chapter 16: The Cover-Up of TWA Flight 800

TWA Flight 800 was a Boeing 747-131 that exploded and crashed into the Atlantic Ocean near East Moriches, New York, on July 17, 1996. The flight was en route from John F. Kennedy International Airport in New York City to Charles de Gaulle Airport in Paris, France. All 230 people on board were killed, making it one of the deadliest aviation accidents in U.S. history. The crash of TWA Flight 800 has been the subject of intense investigation, speculation, and controversy, with many believing that the true cause of the disaster was covered up by the government and other agencies.

The flight took off from JFK at 8:19 p.m. EDT and was climbing to its cruising altitude when, about 12 minutes after takeoff, it suddenly exploded and disintegrated in midair. Eyewitnesses on the ground and at sea reported seeing a streak of light ascending toward the aircraft, followed by an explosion. The wreckage of the plane fell into the ocean, scattering debris over a wide area. The immediate response involved a massive search and rescue operation, but there were no survivors.

The National Transportation Safety Board (NTSB) led the official investigation into the crash, with the assistance of the Federal Bureau of Investigation (FBI) and other agencies. The investigation was one of the most extensive and expensive in aviation history, involving the recovery of wreckage from the ocean floor, analysis of flight data recorders, and numerous tests and simulations. The NTSB's final report, released in 2000, concluded that the probable cause of the crash was an explosion of the center wing fuel tank, likely due to an electrical short circuit that ignited flammable fuel vapors.

Despite the NTSB's conclusion, the investigation into TWA Flight 800 was fraught with controversy and allegations of a cover-up. Some of the key points of contention include the following:

1. **Eyewitness Testimony**: More than 200 eyewitnesses reported seeing a streak of light or missile-like object ascending toward the aircraft before the explosion. These reports were consistent with the idea that the plane was shot down by a missile. The NTSB and FBI interviewed many of these witnesses but ultimately dismissed their accounts as misinterpretations of the events they saw. Critics argue that the eyewitness testimony was not given adequate consideration and that it suggests a possible missile strike.

2. **Physical Evidence**: Some of the wreckage recovered from the ocean showed signs of damage that some experts believe is consistent with a missile strike or external explosion. For example, certain pieces of debris exhibited pitting and holes that could have been caused by high-velocity fragments, a characteristic of a missile explosion. The NTSB's report, however, attributed these markings to the impact forces and post-crash fire.

3. **Radar Data**: Radar data recorded by the FAA and military installations showed unidentified objects in the vicinity of Flight 800 at the time of the explosion. Some analysts believe these objects could have been missiles or other aircraft. The NTSB examined the radar data and concluded that the objects were consistent with debris from the disintegrating aircraft, but skeptics argue that the data indicates a more sinister cause.

4. **Military Exercises**: At the time of the crash, military exercises were being conducted in the area, leading to speculation that Flight 800 was accidentally shot down by a U.S. Navy missile. The U.S. military denied any involvement and stated that no missiles were fired during the exercises. However, the presence of military vessels in the vicinity has fueled suspicions and conspiracy theories.

5. **Government and Media Response**: Critics of the official investigation allege that the government and media were complicit in covering up the true cause of the crash. They argue that the investigation was subject to undue influence and that key evidence was suppressed or ignored. Some believe that the U.S. government had reasons to conceal the true cause, such as avoiding international conflict or protecting sensitive military operations.

In addition to these points of contention, several high-profile figures and organizations have voiced their skepticism about the official findings. Pierre Salinger, a former White House Press Secretary, claimed that Flight 800 was shot down by a U.S. Navy missile and that he had seen a CIA document confirming this. Although Salinger's credibility was questioned and his claims were largely discredited, his assertions added fuel to the conspiracy theories surrounding the crash.

In 1997, a group of independent investigators and aviation experts formed the "Flight 800 Independent Researchers Organization" (FIRO) to conduct their own analysis of the crash. FIRO's members have published numerous articles and reports challenging the NTSB's conclusions and suggesting alternative explanations, including the missile theory. They argue that the evidence points to a cover-up and that the true cause of the disaster has been hidden from the public.

In 2013, several former NTSB investigators who worked on the TWA Flight 800 case filed a petition to reopen the investigation, citing new evidence and advances in forensic technology. They claimed that the original investigation was flawed and that the explosion was likely caused by an external detonation, such as a missile or bomb. The NTSB reviewed the petition but ultimately declined to reopen the case, stating that the new evidence did not provide a basis for changing the original conclusions.

The controversy surrounding TWA Flight 800 has persisted for decades, fueled by the numerous inconsistencies, unanswered questions, and the emotional impact of the tragedy. For the families of the victims, the quest for truth and justice has been a long and painful journey. Many continue to seek answers and hold out hope that new evidence or revelations will one day provide clarity and closure.

The TWA Flight 800 disaster also serves as a case study in the broader context of aviation safety, government transparency, and the challenges of investigating complex accidents. It highlights the difficulties faced by investigators in reconstructing events based on limited and often conflicting evidence. It also underscores the importance of transparency and accountability in maintaining public trust in governmental and investigative institutions.

In popular culture, the crash of TWA Flight 800 has inspired numerous books, documentaries, and fictional portrayals. These works often explore the various theories and controversies, reflecting the enduring fascination and mystery surrounding the event. The story of Flight 800 continues to captivate and provoke debate, illustrating the complex interplay between facts, speculation, and the human desire for understanding and resolution.

Ultimately, the tragedy of TWA Flight 800 is a poignant reminder of the fragility of human life and the enduring impact of sudden and unexplained loss. It challenges us to grapple with the uncertainties and ambiguities of our world, and to strive for greater clarity, honesty, and compassion in the face of tragedy. The legacy of Flight 800 endures as a testament to the resilience of those who seek the truth and the memory of those who lost their lives on that fateful night.

Chapter 17: The Mysterious Death of Kurt Cobain

The mysterious death of Kurt Cobain, the lead singer, guitarist, and primary songwriter of the iconic grunge band Nirvana, has been the subject of widespread speculation, conspiracy theories, and ongoing debates since his tragic passing in 1994. Cobain's untimely death at the age of 27 has been officially ruled a suicide by the authorities, but numerous questions and anomalies surrounding the circumstances of his demise have led many to believe that there might be more to the story.

Kurt Cobain was born on February 20, 1967, in Aberdeen, Washington. He rose to fame in the early 1990s with Nirvana, which became one of the most influential bands of its time, spearheading the grunge movement with their breakthrough album "Nevermind" and its lead single "Smells Like Teen Spirit." Cobain's music was characterized by its raw emotion, powerful lyrics, and a distinctive blend of punk rock and alternative sounds. Despite his success, Cobain struggled with various personal issues, including chronic health problems, substance abuse, and a deep-seated sense of alienation and depression.

On April 8, 1994, Kurt Cobain's body was discovered at his home in Seattle, Washington, by an electrician named Gary Smith who had arrived to install a security system. Cobain was found in a greenhouse above the garage, and it was determined that he had died from a self-inflicted gunshot wound to the head. A shotgun was found resting on his chest, and a suicide note addressed to his wife, Courtney Love, and their daughter, Frances Bean Cobain, was discovered nearby. The note expressed Cobain's inner turmoil and his sense of being overwhelmed by the pressures of fame.

The official cause of death was determined to be suicide, and the medical examiner's report stated that Cobain had died on April 5,

1994. However, from the moment his death was announced, there were those who questioned the official narrative. Over the years, various pieces of evidence, witness statements, and forensic details have been scrutinized, leading to alternative theories that suggest Cobain may have been murdered.

One of the central figures in the conspiracy theories is Tom Grant, a private investigator hired by Courtney Love shortly before Cobain's death to locate her missing husband. Grant has been a vocal critic of the official investigation and has presented several points that he believes indicate foul play. One of the key aspects of Grant's argument is the level of heroin found in Cobain's system at the time of his death. According to the toxicology report, Cobain had a high concentration of heroin, along with traces of diazepam (Valium), in his bloodstream. Grant and other skeptics argue that the amount of heroin present would have incapacitated Cobain to the point where he would not have been able to pull the trigger on the shotgun.

Another point of contention is the suicide note itself. While the majority of the note reads like a farewell letter to Cobain's fans and an explanation of his decision to leave the music industry, the final lines, which directly reference his suicide, appear to be written in a different handwriting style. Some handwriting experts and those close to Cobain have suggested that the final lines were added by someone else, raising suspicions about the note's authenticity. Courtney Love has also been a focal point in the conspiracy theories. Her relationship with Cobain was tumultuous, marked by drug abuse and public confrontations. Some theorists suggest that Love had a motive to have Cobain killed, whether due to financial reasons, personal conflicts, or a desire to gain control over his estate and the rights to his music. These claims have been vehemently denied by Love, who has consistently maintained that Cobain's death was a tragic suicide.

Additionally, there are inconsistencies and unexplained details related to the crime scene. For instance, the position of the shotgun and the lack of fingerprints on the weapon have raised questions. According to the police report, the shotgun was found resting on Cobain's chest, but there were no discernible fingerprints on the gun or the shell casings. This has led some to speculate that the scene may have been staged to look like a suicide. Furthermore, the behavior and actions of certain individuals in the days leading up to and following Cobain's death have been scrutinized. For example, there are discrepancies in the timelines and accounts provided by those who last saw Cobain alive. Additionally, the role of Courtney Love's former boyfriend and musician, El Duce (Eldon Hoke), has been a point of interest. Hoke claimed in a videotaped interview that Love offered him $50,000 to kill Cobain. Although Hoke later passed a polygraph test regarding his allegations, he died under mysterious circumstances shortly after making these claims, further fueling the conspiracy theories.

Despite the numerous questions and alternative theories, the official stance remains that Kurt Cobain died by suicide. The Seattle Police Department has reviewed the case multiple times, including a re-examination of evidence in 2014, but they have consistently upheld the original conclusion. In 2014, previously undeveloped film from the crime scene was released, showing additional photographs of the scene, which authorities stated provided no new information that would change the original ruling.

The cultural and emotional impact of Cobain's death cannot be overstated. As a figurehead of the grunge movement and a voice for a generation, Cobain's music and persona resonated deeply with fans who identified with his struggles and felt a profound sense of loss at his passing. The ongoing debates and theories surrounding his death have only added to his legend, creating a narrative that intertwines tragedy, mystery, and the enduring influence of his work.

Kurt Cobain's legacy continues to be celebrated and analyzed through documentaries, books, and various forms of media. Films such as "Kurt & Courtney" by Nick Broomfield and "Soaked in Bleach" by

Benjamin Statler have explored the conspiracy theories and presented evidence challenging the official account of Cobain's death. These works, while controversial, highlight the enduring fascination with Cobain's life and the unresolved questions surrounding his death.

The case of Kurt Cobain's death also raises broader issues about the nature of fame, mental health, and the pressures faced by public figures. Cobain's struggles with addiction, depression, and the demands of his career are well-documented, and his story has prompted discussions about the support systems available to artists and the importance of addressing mental health issues openly and compassionately.

In the years since his death, Cobain's influence on music and popular culture has only grown. Nirvana's music continues to inspire new generations of musicians and fans, and Cobain's image has become emblematic of the 1990s alternative rock scene. His lyrics, often introspective and raw, offer a glimpse into his troubled mind and the complexities of his experiences, resonating with listeners who find solace and understanding in his words.

Ultimately, the mysterious death of Kurt Cobain remains a topic of intense debate and speculation. While the official ruling of suicide stands, the questions and alternative theories persist, fueled by inconsistencies, unanswered questions, and the enduring allure of Cobain's persona. As time goes on, new evidence and perspectives may emerge, but for now, the full truth of what happened on that fateful day in April 1994 remains elusive.

Chapter 18: The Denver International Airport Conspiracy

The Denver International Airport (DIA) conspiracy is a fascinating amalgamation of myths, suspicions, and elaborate theories that have captivated the minds of many since the airport's construction. Opened in 1995, DIA has been the subject of numerous conspiracy theories that touch on everything from secret underground bunkers to ominous symbols scattered throughout its premises. This narrative has its roots in the unique circumstances surrounding the airport's construction, the peculiar artwork and design choices, and the ongoing mysteries that seem to perpetuate a sense of enigma around this otherwise modern travel hub.

To begin with, the Denver International Airport is vast, sprawling across 33,531 acres, making it the largest airport in the United States by land area. This expanse, combined with its controversial and delayed construction, provided fertile ground for speculation. The airport was completed at a cost of approximately $4.8 billion, far exceeding initial budgets and leading to significant delays. These budget overruns and delays prompted whispers of mismanagement and hidden agendas. Some theorists argue that these were deliberate attempts to cover up the construction of an expansive underground facility, purportedly for use by the global elite in the event of a catastrophe.

One of the most pervasive conspiracy theories surrounding DIA is the idea that it houses a vast network of underground bunkers and tunnels. According to proponents of this theory, the airport's subterranean structures are more than just logistical support areas; they are alleged to be part of a clandestine network that could serve as a sanctuary for members of a shadowy global cabal in times of crisis. Some even suggest that the tunnels connect to the North American Aerospace Defense Command (NORAD) in nearby Colorado

Springs, although no credible evidence has surfaced to support such claims. The extensive underground baggage handling system, which faced significant issues and was eventually abandoned, further fueled these suspicions, with some believing that its true purpose was far more nefarious.

The airport's unique and sometimes unsettling artistic elements have only added to the mystique. The most infamous of these is the 32-foot-tall sculpture of a blue mustang known as "Blucifer" by locals. Officially titled "Mustang," this sculpture, with its glowing red eyes, has been a source of unease for many. The artist, Luis Jiménez, tragically died when a part of the sculpture fell on him during its creation, which only added to the statue's sinister reputation. Some conspiracy theorists interpret the red eyes as a symbol of the Four Horsemen of the Apocalypse or as an indication of a demonic influence.

Inside the terminal, various murals by artist Leo Tanguma have also sparked significant controversy and debate. These murals, with their bold colors and disturbing imagery, depict scenes of war, environmental destruction, and peace. The artwork, meant to convey a message of hope and the triumph of good over evil, has been interpreted by some as displaying a more sinister agenda. One mural, in particular, features a figure in a gas mask, holding a rifle, and appears to be sowing death and destruction, while another part of the mural shows children from various cultures bringing their weapons to be beaten into plowshares by a child in the center, symbolizing a move towards peace. Conspiracy theorists, however, argue that these images are prophetic and represent a hidden, apocalyptic message, or that they signal an impending global catastrophe orchestrated by a secretive elite.

Adding to the air of mystery are various symbols and plaques throughout the airport that have been linked to secret societies. One such plaque, located in the airport's Great Hall, includes a dedication stone with a Masonic symbol, the square and compasses, and references a "New World Airport Commission." This term has fueled speculation about a connection to the New World Order, a theorized global totalitarian government. The inclusion of this symbol, along with the obscure naming of the commission, has led many to believe that the airport is somehow linked to a grander, more nefarious scheme involving Freemasons or other secret societies. In reality, the New World Airport Commission was a local civic organization that helped plan the airport's opening, and the Masonic symbol is a common feature in many public buildings.

The overall design of the airport has also raised eyebrows among conspiracy theorists. The aerial view of the airport's runways has been likened to a swastika, although this is generally considered a coincidence of the layout designed for efficiency and safety. Furthermore, some theorists point to the distinctive white tent-like roof of the main terminal, claiming it resembles Native American teepees or the peaks of the Rocky Mountains, possibly hiding some deeper symbolic meaning. Others suggest that the design is intended to be a beacon or an identifier for extraterrestrial beings, linking the airport to UFO conspiracy theories.

The narrative is also bolstered by the numerous gargoyles that adorn the airport. Perched above baggage claim areas, these stone figures are intended to be whimsical and to play on the idea of protecting travelers' luggage. However, for some, these gargoyles are ominous figures that symbolize hidden demonic influences or secret guardians of the underground complexes.

Interestingly, the airport's administration has taken a rather light-hearted approach to these conspiracy theories. They have even incorporated them into their marketing campaigns, positioning the airport as a quirky and mysterious destination. Tours have been offered that highlight the various features and artwork that have sparked these theories, turning what some see as ominous signs into a unique attraction for the curious and the skeptical alike.

Despite the airport's efforts to debunk the theories and demystify its premises, the legend of the Denver International Airport conspiracy persists. It serves as a potent example of how modern architecture, combined with a touch of artistic whimsy and a few unfortunate coincidences, can give rise to a complex web of myths and intrigue. The ongoing fascination with DIA highlights a broader human tendency to find patterns and meaning in ambiguous or unusual circumstances, and to weave narratives that reflect deeper anxieties about power, secrecy, and the unknown.

Chapter 19: The Death of Tupac Shakur

The death of Tupac Shakur, one of the most iconic and influential rappers of all time, has been shrouded in mystery and controversy for nearly three decades. On September 7, 1996, Tupac was shot multiple times in a drive-by shooting in Las Vegas, Nevada. He succumbed to his injuries six days later, on September 13, at the age of 25. Despite the passage of time, the circumstances surrounding his death remain a fertile ground for conspiracy theories, speculation, and debate. The mystery is further compounded by Tupac's complex persona, his contentious relationships within the music industry, and the socio-political environment of the 1990s.

Tupac Shakur, born Lesane Parish Crooks on June 16, 1971, and later renamed Tupac Amaru Shakur, was a multifaceted artist whose work spanned music, film, and activism. His life was marked by a deep engagement with the struggles of African Americans, the injustices of the American legal system, and the contradictions of fame and success. Shakur's music often delved into themes of violence, poverty, and racial discrimination, making him a voice for the marginalized and a target for controversy.

On the night of his shooting, Tupac was in Las Vegas to attend a boxing match between Mike Tyson and Bruce Seldon at the MGM Grand. Accompanied by Marion "Suge" Knight, the CEO of Death Row Records, Tupac was involved in a scuffle with a gang member, Orlando "Baby Lane" Anderson, in the hotel lobby after the fight. This altercation is widely believed to be connected to the events that unfolded later that night. After leaving the MGM Grand, Tupac and Suge Knight headed to Club 662, a nightclub owned by Knight, where they planned to attend a party.

While en route to the club, a white Cadillac pulled up alongside the black BMW in which Tupac and Knight were traveling. The occupants of the Cadillac opened fire, hitting Tupac four times, twice in the chest, once in the arm, and once in the thigh. Suge Knight was grazed by a bullet but survived with minor injuries. Tupac was rushed to the University Medical Center of Southern Nevada, where he was placed in a medically induced coma. Despite undergoing multiple surgeries, he died of respiratory failure and cardiac arrest on September 13, 1996.

The immediate aftermath of Tupac's death saw a flurry of speculation and finger-pointing. The Las Vegas Metropolitan Police Department launched an investigation, but it quickly stalled due to a lack of cooperation from witnesses and an absence of concrete leads. Various theories emerged, attempting to explain who might have been responsible for the shooting and why. Among the most prominent suspects was Orlando Anderson, the Crips gang member involved in the scuffle with Tupac at the MGM Grand. Anderson denied any involvement and was never charged in connection with the shooting. He was later killed in an unrelated gang dispute in 1998.

Another major theory implicates Suge Knight himself, who was in the car with Tupac at the time of the shooting. Some speculate that Knight had Tupac killed to prevent him from leaving Death Row Records, as Tupac had reportedly expressed a desire to start his own label. Proponents of this theory argue that Knight's minor injuries in the shooting could indicate he was not the intended target. However, no credible evidence has ever emerged to support these claims, and Knight has consistently denied any involvement in Tupac's death.

The involvement of the FBI and other law enforcement agencies has also been a subject of speculation. Some theories suggest that Tupac was targeted by the government due to his influence and his ties to the Black Panther Party, an organization to which his mother, Afeni Shakur, was a prominent member. These theories often cite COINTELPRO, an FBI program aimed at surveilling, infiltrating, and discrediting African American political organizations, as evidence of a potential motive. However, these claims remain speculative, with no concrete evidence linking the FBI or other government agencies to Tupac's murder.

One of the most persistent and intriguing theories surrounding Tupac's death is that he faked his own demise and is living in hiding. This theory is fueled by numerous purported sightings of Tupac in various locations around the world, as well as by his posthumous releases. Tupac's ability to release a steady stream of new music long after his death has led some to believe that he is still alive and continuing to record in secret. Supporters of this theory point to various inconsistencies in the official account of Tupac's death, such as the lack of a public autopsy report and the swift cremation of his body. Despite the allure of this theory, there is no credible evidence to suggest that Tupac is alive, and it is widely regarded as a piece of modern mythology.

The East Coast-West Coast rivalry in the hip-hop world during the 1990s provides another context for understanding the conspiracies surrounding Tupac's death. This rivalry, which pitted artists and record labels from the East Coast, particularly New York, against their counterparts on the West Coast, primarily Los Angeles, was marked by intense feuds, diss tracks, and, at times, violent confrontations. Tupac was a prominent figure on the West Coast, signed to Death Row Records, while his rival, Christopher "The Notorious B.I.G." Wallace, was a leading figure on the East Coast, signed to Bad Boy Records. The rivalry between Tupac and Biggie is often cited as a potential factor in their untimely deaths, with some theories suggesting that Biggie or his associates may have been involved in the Las Vegas shooting. However, no substantial evidence has emerged to support these claims, and Biggie himself was murdered in a drive-by shooting in Los Angeles just six months after Tupac's death, further complicating the narrative.

Adding to the mystery is the role of Death Row Records, a label known for its ties to gang culture and its involvement in numerous legal battles. Suge Knight, the label's head, has been a controversial figure, often linked to violent incidents and criminal activities. Some theories suggest that internal conflicts within Death Row, including financial disputes and power struggles, could have played a role in Tupac's death. There is also speculation that the record label's connections to the Bloods gang could have led to retaliatory actions from rival gangs, contributing to the atmosphere of violence and mistrust that surrounded Tupac in his final days.

Tupac's own persona and lifestyle have also been scrutinized in the context of his death. Known for his confrontational and outspoken nature, Tupac had numerous enemies and was involved in several high-profile feuds. His lyrics often reflected a sense of fatalism and awareness of his own mortality, with songs like "Hail Mary" and "I Ain't Mad at Cha" foreshadowing his death. Some believe that Tupac's public persona and his connections to the criminal underworld made him a target, while others argue that his death was a tragic result of the violent environment he was immersed in.

The enduring legacy of Tupac Shakur adds another layer of complexity to the mystery of his death. His influence on music, culture, and politics remains profound, with his work continuing to inspire new generations of artists and activists. Tupac's ability to articulate the struggles and aspirations of marginalized communities has cemented his status as a cultural icon, and his death has only amplified his mythos. The ongoing fascination with his life and death reflects a broader societal interest in the intersections of art, identity, and power, as well as a deep-seated desire to find meaning in the midst of tragedy.

Chapter 20: The Knights Templar Secrets

The Knights Templar, officially known as the Poor Fellow-Soldiers of Christ and of the Temple of Solomon, were a medieval Christian military order founded in 1119. They were originally established to protect Christian pilgrims traveling to the Holy Land, but over time, they evolved into one of the most powerful and enigmatic organizations of the Middle Ages. The Templars' rise to power, their sudden fall, and the lingering mysteries surrounding them have given rise to countless legends, conspiracy theories, and secretive lore that continue to captivate imaginations today.

The Knights Templar were founded in the aftermath of the First Crusade, a military campaign launched by European Christians to recapture Jerusalem and other sacred sites from Muslim control. The order was created by a French nobleman, Hugues de Payens, and eight of his companions, who took monastic vows of poverty, chastity, and obedience. They established their headquarters on the Temple Mount in Jerusalem, which was believed to be the site of the biblical Temple of Solomon. This location would later contribute to the mystique and speculation surrounding the order.

Initially, the Templars were a small and relatively obscure group, but they quickly gained recognition and support from influential figures in both the Church and European nobility. In 1129, the order received formal endorsement from the Catholic Church at the Council of Troyes, and they were granted the distinctive white mantle adorned with a red cross that would become their iconic symbol. The Templars' military prowess and their role in protecting pilgrims made them a valuable asset to the Crusader states in the Holy Land, and they soon amassed significant wealth and influence.

The Templars' growing wealth and power were primarily derived from their involvement in finance and commerce. Contrary to the popular image of medieval knights as solely warriors, the Templars developed a sophisticated network of banking and financial services. They established a system of letters of credit, which allowed pilgrims and merchants to deposit money in one location and withdraw it in another, thus reducing the risk of robbery during long journeys. This innovative financial system made the Templars the medieval equivalent of an international banking corporation and contributed to their immense wealth.

The order's vast resources enabled them to construct fortifications, acquire land, and maintain a formidable military presence throughout Europe and the Holy Land. However, their financial success and autonomy also attracted envy and suspicion from both secular and religious authorities. The Templars' secretive nature and their rapid rise to power fueled rumors of hidden knowledge and forbidden practices, setting the stage for the myths and conspiracies that would later envelop their legacy.

One of the most enduring mysteries associated with the Templars is the question of their supposed hidden treasures and secret knowledge. According to legend, the Templars uncovered ancient secrets and sacred relics during their time in the Holy Land. Some accounts suggest that they discovered the Ark of the Covenant or the Holy Grail, the cup believed to have been used by Jesus Christ at the Last Supper. These relics, if they existed, would have bestowed immense spiritual and temporal power upon the order. However, there is no historical evidence to support these claims, and they remain the stuff of legend and speculation.

The Templars' downfall was as dramatic and sudden as their rise to power. By the early 14th century, the Crusader states in the Holy Land had been lost to Muslim forces, and the Templars' original mission was no longer relevant. Their vast wealth and influence made them a target for the French king, Philip IV, who was deeply in debt to the order. In 1307, Philip launched a campaign to dismantle the Templars, arresting their leaders and accusing them of heresy, blasphemy, and other crimes.

The accusations included charges of idol worship, sacrilegious rituals, and sexual misconduct, many of which were likely fabricated or exaggerated.

Under torture, many Templars confessed to these charges, although the confessions were later retracted. Nevertheless, the confessions provided the pretext for a widespread crackdown on the order. In 1312, Pope Clement V, under pressure from Philip, officially disbanded the Templars at the Council of Vienne, and their assets were confiscated by the Church and secular authorities. The last Grand Master of the order, Jacques de Molay, was burned at the stake in 1314, maintaining his innocence and cursing his persecutors with his dying breath.

The dramatic suppression of the Templars, coupled with the enigmatic nature of their organization, gave rise to a plethora of conspiracy theories and myths. One of the most famous theories is that the Templars went underground and continued to exist in secret, influencing world events from the shadows. This idea has been popularized in modern times by works of fiction such as Dan Brown's "The Da Vinci Code," which portrays the Templars as guardians of ancient secrets and hidden knowledge.

Another widely debated aspect of Templar lore is their supposed connection to Freemasonry. Some theorists argue that the Templars, after their disbandment, went into hiding and eventually resurfaced as the Freemasons, a fraternal organization that emerged in the 17th and 18th centuries. Proponents of this theory point to similarities in symbols and rituals between the two groups, as well as the Freemasons' reverence for the Temple of Solomon. However, historians generally consider this connection to be speculative and unsupported by concrete evidence.

The Templars are also frequently linked to the mysteries of Rosslyn Chapel in Scotland. Built in the 15th century, Rosslyn Chapel is renowned for its intricate stone carvings and alleged hidden symbolism. Some believe that the chapel contains hidden Templar treasures or secrets, including the Holy Grail or the Ark of the Covenant. This theory is bolstered by the fact that the chapel's founders, the Sinclair family, were known to have connections with the Templars. However, like many aspects of Templar lore, these claims are largely based on speculation and interpretation rather than verifiable historical facts.

The Knights Templar have also been associated with various esoteric and occult traditions. Some theories suggest that the Templars were custodians of ancient mystical knowledge or that they practiced secret rituals derived from Gnostic or Hermetic traditions. These theories often portray the Templars as part of a hidden lineage of spiritual seekers or as guardians of secret wisdom that predates Christianity. While such ideas are intriguing, they are not supported by historical evidence and are often the product of modern occultism and speculative fiction.

The Templars' supposed involvement in alchemy, the quest for the Philosopher's Stone, and the pursuit of hidden wisdom have also contributed to their mystique. Alchemy, the medieval precursor to chemistry, was often associated with the search for spiritual enlightenment and the transformation of base metals into gold. Some theories propose that the Templars possessed alchemical knowledge or that they were engaged in secret experiments to discover the secrets of the universe. While these ideas are largely speculative, they reflect the broader fascination with the Templars as keepers of hidden knowledge and mystical secrets.

The enduring allure of the Knights Templar lies in their combination of historical fact and tantalizing mystery. Their rise and fall provide a dramatic narrative, while their wealth, power, and secrecy fuel endless speculation about their true nature and purpose. Whether seen as noble warriors, secretive conspirators, or mystical seekers, the Templars continue to captivate the imagination and inspire a rich tapestry of myths, legends, and theories.

In modern times, the legacy of the Knights Templar has been embraced by various groups and movements. From neo-Templar organizations that claim to uphold the values of the original order to conspiracy theorists who see the Templars as key players in a hidden global agenda, the Templars remain a powerful symbol of mystery and intrigue. Their story resonates with themes of power, betrayal, and the search for hidden truths, making them a compelling subject for both historical inquiry and imaginative speculation.

Chapter 21: The Bilderberg Group Meetings

The Bilderberg Group, a highly secretive and exclusive annual gathering, has been the subject of intense speculation and numerous conspiracy theories since its inception in 1954. Comprising influential figures from the realms of politics, business, finance, academia, and the media, the group's meetings are closed to the public and media, fueling suspicions about their motives and objectives. The group's alleged role in shaping global policy and steering world events from behind the scenes has made it a focal point for those who believe in the existence of a powerful, shadowy elite. This detailed exploration of the Bilderberg Group aims to shed light on its origins, operations, controversies, and the myths that surround it.

The Bilderberg Group was founded by Dutch politician Joseph Retinger, who was concerned about the growing divide between the United States and Western Europe during the early years of the Cold War. He believed that fostering greater understanding and cooperation between influential leaders from both sides of the Atlantic would help to counter the threat posed by the Soviet Union and ensure the stability of the Western world. Retinger's vision was supported by Prince Bernhard of the Netherlands, and the first meeting of the group took place at the Hotel de Bilderberg in Oosterbeek, Netherlands, from May 29 to 31, 1954, giving the group its name.

The stated purpose of the Bilderberg Group is to facilitate informal discussions on a wide range of topics, including international relations, economic issues, and global security. The meetings are designed to foster candid and open dialogue among participants, who attend in a private capacity rather than as official representatives of their countries or organizations. This approach is intended to promote the free exchange of ideas and to encourage the development of mutual understanding and cooperation. However, the group's policy of strict confidentiality, with no minutes or reports made public, has led to accusations of secrecy and a lack of transparency, which in turn has fueled conspiracy theories about its true intentions.

Each year, the Bilderberg Group invites around 120 to 150 participants, who are selected by a steering committee made up of prominent members from various countries. The invitees are typically drawn from a pool of political leaders, top executives from major corporations, leading academics, and influential figures from the media. The exact criteria for selection are not publicly disclosed, but it is widely believed that participants are chosen based on their ability to contribute to the discussions and their potential influence on public policy and opinion. The meetings are held in different locations each year, often at luxury hotels or resorts, and the exact agenda is kept confidential.

The secrecy surrounding the Bilderberg meetings has given rise to numerous conspiracy theories, many of which claim that the group is a tool for the manipulation of world events by a powerful elite. One of the most persistent theories is that the Bilderberg Group serves as a front for a secretive cabal that seeks to establish a New World Order, a concept that refers to a centralized, authoritarian global government. Proponents of this theory argue that the group's discussions and decisions are aimed at consolidating power and control over key aspects of global affairs, including finance, politics, and the media. They believe that the Bilderberg Group's members use their influence to shape policy and steer world events in ways that benefit their interests at the expense of ordinary people.

Another popular theory is that the Bilderberg Group plays a key role in selecting and grooming future political leaders. Some conspiracy theorists point to the presence of prominent politicians at Bilderberg meetings shortly before they rose to power as evidence that the group has a hand in orchestrating political careers. For example, Bill Clinton attended a Bilderberg meeting in 1991, the year before he announced his candidacy for the U.S. presidency, and Tony Blair attended a meeting in 1993, shortly before becoming the leader of the UK Labour Party. While it is true that many influential leaders have participated in Bilderberg meetings, there is no concrete evidence to suggest that the group actively manipulates political appointments or elections.

The Bilderberg Group's alleged influence over economic policy is another area of concern for conspiracy theorists. Critics argue that the group's discussions often focus on issues related to global finance and trade, and that its members include some of the most powerful figures in the business world. They claim that the group uses its meetings to coordinate strategies that favor large multinational corporations and financial institutions, often at the expense of smaller businesses and national economies. This has led to accusations that the Bilderberg Group is part of a larger effort to establish a global economic system that is controlled by a few powerful entities.

One of the most controversial aspects of the Bilderberg Group is its lack of transparency and accountability. The group's meetings are closed to the public and the media, and there are no official records or minutes available for scrutiny. This has led to criticism from various quarters, including politicians, journalists, and activists, who argue that the group's activities should be subject to greater oversight. Some have called for the Bilderberg meetings to be opened up to public scrutiny or for the group to provide more detailed information about its discussions and decisions. However, the Bilderberg Group has consistently defended its policy of confidentiality, arguing that it is necessary to facilitate frank and open dialogue among participants.

The lack of transparency has also led to speculation about the specific topics discussed at Bilderberg meetings and the potential impact of these discussions on global policy. While the group does release a general agenda for each meeting, the details of the discussions and the outcomes are not made public. This has led to concerns that the group may be influencing policy decisions in ways that are not subject to democratic oversight or accountability. Critics argue that the Bilderberg Group's meetings provide an opportunity for powerful individuals to coordinate strategies and make decisions that affect the lives of millions of people without any input from the public or elected representatives.

Despite the secrecy and controversy, it is important to recognize that the Bilderberg Group is not a monolithic entity with a single agenda. The group comprises a diverse range of individuals with different backgrounds, perspectives, and interests, and it is unlikely that they all share the same goals or views. While it is possible that some participants may use the meetings to advance their own agendas, it is also likely that many attendees genuinely seek to foster dialogue and cooperation on important global issues. The group's impact on policy and world events is difficult to assess, given the lack of transparency, but it is important to approach the subject with a critical and balanced perspective.

The history of the Bilderberg Group's meetings provides some insight into the evolution of its role and influence. In the early years, the group's discussions focused primarily on issues related to the Cold War and the relationship between the United States and Western Europe. Topics included the threat of communism, the need for greater economic and political cooperation, and the challenges of maintaining security and stability in a rapidly changing world. Over time, the scope of the discussions expanded to include a wider range of issues, such as globalization, environmental sustainability, and the impact of technology on society.

In recent years, the Bilderberg Group's meetings have addressed some of the most pressing challenges facing the world today, including climate change, cyber security, and the rise of populism and nationalism. The group's agenda often reflects current geopolitical trends and concerns, and the discussions are likely to influence the perspectives and decisions of the participants. However, it is important to note that the Bilderberg Group does not have any formal decision-making authority, and its discussions are intended to be informal and advisory rather than prescriptive.

The media's coverage of the Bilderberg Group has also played a significant role in shaping public perceptions of the group. The secretive nature of the meetings and the high-profile participants have made the group a popular target for journalists and investigators seeking to uncover hidden truths. Over the years, numerous books, articles, and documentaries have been produced that claim to reveal the inner workings of the Bilderberg Group and its alleged influence over world events. While some of these works provide valuable insights and raise important questions, others rely on speculation and unverified information, contributing to the mythologizing of the group.

The Bilderberg Group's critics often point to the lack of diversity among its participants as evidence of its elitist and exclusionary nature. The group has been criticized for being dominated by wealthy, white, male participants from Western countries, with limited representation from women, minorities, and developing nations. This lack of diversity raises questions about the perspectives and interests that are represented at the meetings and the extent to which the group's discussions reflect the concerns and needs of the broader global population. Efforts to address these concerns have included calls for greater transparency, accountability, and inclusivity in the selection of participants and the topics discussed.

Chapter 22: The Disappearance of the Mary Celeste

The disappearance of the Mary Celeste is one of the most enduring maritime mysteries in history. The tale of this ghost ship, found abandoned in the Atlantic Ocean in 1872, has fascinated and perplexed people for over a century. Despite extensive investigations and numerous theories, the true fate of the Mary Celeste and her crew remains a subject of speculation and intrigue. This detailed exploration will delve into the background of the ship, the circumstances of its discovery, the various theories proposed over the years, and the continuing legacy of this enigmatic case.

The Mary Celeste, originally named the Amazon, was a 282-ton brigantine built in Nova Scotia, Canada, in 1861. The ship had a troubled history from the beginning. During its maiden voyage, the captain fell ill and died, and the ship suffered various mishaps and accidents over the years, leading to a reputation for being cursed. After changing hands several times, it was finally acquired by American owners and renamed the Mary Celeste in 1869.

In November 1872, the Mary Celeste set sail from New York City bound for Genoa, Italy, under the command of Captain Benjamin Briggs, a highly respected and experienced mariner. Onboard were seven crew members, Captain Briggs' wife Sarah, and their two-year-old daughter, Sophia. The ship was carrying a cargo of 1,701 barrels of denatured alcohol, a type of industrial ethanol, which was being shipped to a consortium of Italian merchants.

The Mary Celeste's voyage appeared to proceed uneventfully until December 4, 1872, when it was spotted adrift in the Atlantic Ocean by the British brigantine Dei Gratia, commanded by Captain David Morehouse. The Dei Gratia had left New York City eight days after the Mary Celeste and was following a similar route to Europe. Upon sighting the Mary Celeste, Captain Morehouse and his crew became concerned when they saw that the ship was sailing erratically and did not respond to their signals. Fearing that the vessel was in distress, Morehouse sent a boarding party to investigate.

When the crew of the Dei Gratia boarded the Mary Celeste, they found the ship completely abandoned. There was no sign of Captain Briggs, his family, or the crew. The ship's cargo of alcohol was largely intact, and there was no evidence of a struggle or foul play. The lifeboat was missing, and the ship's only compass had been broken, but otherwise, the Mary Celeste was seaworthy and in good condition. The boarding party also discovered that the ship's chronometer and sextant were missing, along with the ship's papers, except for the captain's logbook, which recorded the ship's position and course up to November 25, 1872.

The crew of the Dei Gratia sailed the Mary Celeste to Gibraltar, where an official inquiry was conducted by the British authorities. The inquiry found no evidence of piracy or foul play and ruled out the possibility that the crew had abandoned ship in a panic. The Mary Celeste's cargo was inspected, and it was found that nine of the barrels of alcohol were empty, but there was no indication that this had been a factor in the crew's disappearance. Despite extensive investigations, the fate of the crew remained a mystery, and the case was closed without a definitive conclusion.

The discovery of the Mary Celeste and the mysterious disappearance of its crew have given rise to numerous theories over the years, each attempting to explain what might have happened. One of the earliest and most enduring theories is that the crew abandoned ship due to fears of an explosion or poisoning from the cargo of alcohol. Denatured alcohol is highly volatile and can produce toxic fumes, and it is possible that the crew noticed a leak or detected the smell of alcohol, leading them to fear for their safety. In this scenario, the crew may have taken to the lifeboat, intending to return once the danger had passed, but were subsequently lost at sea.

Another theory suggests that the crew may have encountered a severe storm or waterspout, which could have caused them to believe that the ship was in imminent danger of sinking. There are reports of heavy weather in the area around the time the Mary Celeste disappeared, and it is possible that a sudden and violent storm could have caused the crew to abandon ship in a panic. However, this theory is undermined by the fact that the ship was found largely undamaged and seaworthy, with no signs of having encountered severe weather.

Some theorists have proposed that the Mary Celeste may have fallen victim to piracy or mutiny. Piracy was not uncommon in the 19th century, and it is possible that the ship was attacked by pirates who subsequently abandoned it after failing to find valuable plunder. Alternatively, the crew may have mutinied and overpowered Captain Briggs, taking the lifeboat in an attempt to escape. However, there is no evidence of a struggle or violence on board the ship, and the valuable cargo was left untouched, making these theories less likely.

A more outlandish theory is that the Mary Celeste was the victim of a supernatural or extraterrestrial event. Some have speculated that the crew was abducted by aliens or that the ship encountered some otherworldly phenomenon that caused the crew to vanish. This theory, while intriguing, is not supported by any evidence and remains firmly in the realm of fiction.

Another possibility is that the crew may have been struck down by a sudden and mysterious illness or poisoning. There are reports that the Mary Celeste's water supply was contaminated, and it is possible that the crew succumbed to illness or poisoning, leading them to abandon ship in a desperate attempt to reach help. However, no signs of illness or poisoning were found on the ship, and this theory remains speculative.

One of the most plausible theories is that the crew may have abandoned ship after mistakenly believing that the vessel was sinking. It is possible that a combination of factors, such as a malfunctioning pump or a sudden influx of water, caused the crew to fear that the ship was taking on water and would soon sink. In their panic, they may have taken to the lifeboat, intending to return once the danger had passed, but were subsequently lost at sea. This theory is supported by the fact that the ship's logbook recorded a series of unusual readings and entries in the days leading up to the crew's disappearance, suggesting that the crew may have been struggling with navigation and other issues.

The mystery of the Mary Celeste has also been the subject of numerous fictional works, including novels, films, and television shows. One of the earliest fictional accounts was written by Sir Arthur Conan Doyle, the creator of Sherlock Holmes, in 1884. His short story "J. Habakuk Jephson's Statement" presented a sensationalized and fictionalized version of the Mary Celeste's story, in which the ship was found adrift with its crew missing under mysterious circumstances. The story captured the public's imagination and helped to cement the Mary Celeste's place in popular culture as one of the greatest maritime mysteries of all time.

In the years since the Mary Celeste was found adrift, the ship itself has had a checkered and often troubled history. After being returned to her American owners, the ship continued to operate as a cargo vessel, but she was plagued by bad luck and misfortune. The Mary Celeste changed hands several times and was involved in various accidents and mishaps, leading to a reputation for being cursed. In 1885, the ship was deliberately wrecked off the coast of Haiti in an attempt to collect insurance money, but the scheme was discovered, and the ship's final owner was convicted of insurance fraud.

The legacy of the Mary Celeste continues to captivate and intrigue people to this day. The story of the abandoned ship and the missing crew has become a symbol of the mysteries of the sea and the unknown dangers that lie in wait for those who venture into the vast and uncharted waters. The case has inspired countless theories and investigations, each seeking to uncover the truth behind one of the most enduring maritime mysteries in history. Despite the passage of time and the advances in technology and knowledge, the fate of the Mary Celeste and her crew remains an enigma, a testament to the enduring allure of the unknown and the unexplained.

Chapter 23: The Loch Ness Monster Sightings

The Loch Ness Monster, affectionately known as "Nessie," has captivated the imaginations of people around the world for nearly a century. Nestled in the Scottish Highlands, Loch Ness is a vast, deep freshwater loch that stretches approximately 23 miles in length and is over 750 feet deep, making it one of the largest bodies of freshwater in the British Isles. Its dark, murky waters and the surrounding mist-shrouded hills have provided a perfect setting for one of the most enduring and enigmatic legends in modern history. The story of the Loch Ness Monster, replete with mysterious sightings, photographs, and various scientific investigations, is a fascinating tale that blends folklore, science, and a sense of wonder about the unknown.

The legend of the Loch Ness Monster dates back to ancient times, with the earliest references found in Scottish folklore. Local tales spoke of water creatures and supernatural beings inhabiting the loch and other bodies of water in the region. One of the earliest recorded accounts of a strange creature in Loch Ness appears in the seventh-century hagiography of Saint Columba. According to this account, Saint Columba encountered a beast in the River Ness, which flows from the loch, and miraculously saved a man from its clutches by invoking the name of God. While this story may have been intended to highlight the saint's miraculous powers, it also suggests that the idea of a mysterious creature in Loch Ness has ancient roots.

The modern era of Loch Ness Monster sightings began in the early 20th century, with a flurry of reports that catapulted Nessie to worldwide fame. The most significant of these sightings occurred in 1933, when George Spicer and his wife reported seeing a large, strange creature crossing the road in front of their car near the loch. They described the creature as having a large body, a long neck, and no visible limbs. This sighting, widely reported in the press, sparked a surge of interest and curiosity about the possibility of a large, unidentified creature inhabiting the loch.

Later in 1933, a photograph taken by Hugh Gray showed a blurry image of an object in the water that some interpreted as a long-necked creature. Although the photograph was of poor quality and could not conclusively identify the object, it fueled further speculation and excitement. The following year, in 1934, the most famous and controversial photograph of the Loch Ness Monster was taken by Robert Kenneth Wilson, a London gynecologist. Known as the "Surgeon's Photograph," this image appeared to show a long-necked creature rising out of the water. The photograph quickly became iconic and was widely believed to be the best evidence of Nessie's existence.

However, the Surgeon's Photograph was later revealed to be a hoax. In 1994, one of the perpetrators, Christian Spurling, confessed that the photograph was staged using a toy submarine fitted with a model of a creature's head and neck. Despite this revelation, the photograph remains one of the most enduring and famous images associated with the Loch Ness Monster, illustrating the deep-seated fascination and willingness to believe in the existence of such a creature.

Throughout the 20th century, numerous sightings and reports of the Loch Ness Monster continued to emerge, with people from all walks of life claiming to have seen a large, mysterious creature in the loch. These sightings varied widely in their descriptions, with some witnesses reporting a long-necked creature similar to a plesiosaur, while others described a more serpentine or fish-like appearance. Many of these reports were accompanied by photographs or video footage, although most were either of poor quality or could be attributed to more mundane explanations such as waves, floating debris, or known animals like seals or otters.

In addition to eyewitness accounts, several scientific investigations have been conducted to search for evidence of the Loch Ness Monster.

In the 1960s, the Loch Ness Phenomena Investigation Bureau (LNPIB) was formed to conduct systematic searches and gather data about the creature. Using a variety of techniques, including sonar and underwater photography, the LNPIB conducted extensive surveys of the loch but failed to find conclusive evidence of a large, unknown animal. Despite the lack of definitive proof, the group's efforts helped to maintain public interest in the mystery and inspired further scientific inquiries.

One of the most notable scientific investigations took place in 1972, when a team from the Academy of Applied Science, led by Dr. Robert Rines, conducted a series of underwater surveys using sonar and underwater cameras. During their investigations, the team captured several intriguing images, including one that appeared to show the flipper of a large, unknown animal. Although the photographs were of poor quality and subject to various interpretations, they sparked renewed interest in the possibility of a large, unidentified creature inhabiting Loch Ness. Subsequent sonar surveys conducted in the 1980s and 1990s also detected large, moving objects in the loch, but these findings were inconclusive and did not provide definitive evidence of a creature's existence.

In the 21st century, the search for the Loch Ness Monster has continued, with advancements in technology enabling more sophisticated investigations. In 2003, the BBC conducted a comprehensive sonar survey of the loch using 600 separate sonar beams and satellite tracking. The survey, which covered the entire loch, found no evidence of a large, unknown creature and concluded that the Loch Ness Monster was likely a myth. However, proponents of the monster's existence argue that the survey's methods and scope may not have been sufficient to detect a creature that could evade detection in the vast and complex environment of the loch.

One of the most recent and comprehensive investigations into the Loch Ness Monster was conducted in 2018 by a team of scientists led by Professor Neil Gemmell of the University of Otago in New Zealand. The team conducted a DNA survey of the loch's waters, analyzing genetic material to identify the various species present in the ecosystem. The results of the survey revealed the presence of a wide variety of species, including fish, birds, and mammals, but found no evidence of any large, unknown animals. The team did, however, detect significant amounts of eel DNA, leading to speculation that sightings of the Loch Ness Monster could be attributed to large eels, which are known to inhabit the loch and can grow to considerable sizes.

Despite the lack of conclusive scientific evidence, the legend of the Loch Ness Monster remains deeply ingrained in popular culture and continues to attract interest and speculation. The mystery of Nessie has inspired countless books, documentaries, films, and even scientific debates, making it one of the most famous and enduring legends of the modern era. The Loch Ness Monster has become a symbol of the unknown and the unexplored, representing the human fascination with the mysteries of the natural world and the possibility that there may still be creatures lurking in the depths that have yet to be discovered.

The continuing allure of the Loch Ness Monster can be attributed to several factors. First and foremost is the enigmatic nature of Loch Ness itself. The loch's vast size, great depth, and dark, murky waters create an environment that seems perfectly suited to hide a large, elusive creature. The loch's remoteness and the often misty, atmospheric conditions of the surrounding landscape contribute to a sense of mystery and intrigue, making it easy to imagine that something unknown could be lurking beneath the surface.

Another factor is the sheer volume of sightings and reports over the years. While many of these can be explained by natural phenomena or misidentifications, the consistency of certain descriptions, such as the long neck and humped back, suggests that there may be a kernel of truth to the legend. The persistence of these reports, combined with the lack of definitive proof either for or against the monster's existence, keeps the mystery alive and fuels ongoing interest and speculation.

The Loch Ness Monster also holds a special place in the human imagination as a symbol of the unknown and the unexplored. In an age where much of the world has been mapped and studied, the idea that there could still be undiscovered creatures lurking in the depths of Loch Ness captures the imagination and inspires a sense of wonder. The legend of Nessie reminds us that there are still mysteries to be uncovered and that the natural world holds many secrets that have yet to be revealed.

Moreover, the Loch Ness Monster has become a cultural icon and a significant part of Scotland's heritage. The monster has become a symbol of the region and a major tourist attraction, drawing visitors from around the world who hope to catch a glimpse of the elusive creature or simply to experience the beauty and mystery of Loch Ness. The legend of Nessie has also been embraced by the local community, with numerous businesses, attractions, and events celebrating the monster and its enduring legacy.

The story of the Loch Ness Monster has also had a significant impact on the field of cryptozoology, the study of creatures whose existence is based on anecdotal evidence and folklore rather than scientific proof. The search for Nessie has inspired generations of cryptozoologists and researchers to investigate other mysterious creatures and unexplained phenomena around the world. While many of these investigations have been met with skepticism by the scientific community, they reflect a broader human desire to explore the unknown and to believe that there may still be mysteries waiting to be uncovered.

Chapter 24: The Secrets of the Vatican

The Vatican, officially known as the Vatican City State, is the smallest independent city-state in the world, both in terms of area and population. Nestled within the city of Rome, Italy, the Vatican is not only the spiritual and administrative center of the Roman Catholic Church but also a place shrouded in mystery and intrigue. For centuries, it has been a focal point of religious, political, and cultural significance, with a history rich in power, secrecy, and controversy. The secrets of the Vatican encompass a wide range of topics, including its vast archives, secretive political maneuverings, unexplained mysteries, and centuries-old traditions that continue to captivate the world. This detailed exploration delves into the various aspects of the Vatican's secrets, offering an in-depth look at the hidden facets of this enigmatic institution.

The Vatican's origins date back to the early Christian era, when it was established as the seat of the Roman Catholic Church. The area now known as Vatican City was originally a marshy region on the west bank of the Tiber River. According to tradition, Saint Peter, one of Jesus Christ's apostles and the first Pope, was martyred and buried there around 64 AD. Over time, a basilica was constructed over his supposed burial site, marking the beginning of the Vatican's religious significance. By the 4th century, under Emperor Constantine the Great, the Old Saint Peter's Basilica was built, solidifying the Vatican's status as a major Christian pilgrimage site.

In the centuries that followed, the Vatican grew in both size and influence. It became the epicenter of the Catholic Church, and by the 15th century, the Papal States, a group of territories in central Italy ruled by the Pope, had emerged as a significant political and religious power. The construction of the new Saint Peter's Basilica, one of the largest and most impressive churches in the world, began in the 16th century under Pope Julius II and was completed over a span of 120 years. The basilica, along with the Apostolic Palace, the Sistine Chapel, and the Vatican Museums, became central to the Vatican's identity.

One of the most enduring and intriguing aspects of the Vatican is its extensive archives, known as the Vatican Secret Archives. Despite its ominous-sounding name, the "secret" in this context actually refers to the Latin word "secretum," meaning "private" or "personal." These archives contain an immense collection of documents, manuscripts, and letters spanning over a millennium of history, providing a detailed record of the Church's activities, decisions, and correspondences. The archives are housed in a fortified building within the Vatican and are accessible only to a select group of scholars and researchers.

Among the treasures of the Vatican Archives are countless historically significant documents. One of the most famous is the Codex Vaticanus, an ancient manuscript of the Bible written in Greek dating back to the 4th century. It is one of the oldest and most complete texts of the Bible in existence. The archives also contain the correspondence of popes, including letters from figures such as Michelangelo, King Henry VIII, and Martin Luther. These documents provide invaluable insights into the history of the Catholic Church and its interactions with the wider world.

Despite its vast historical importance, access to the Vatican Archives is highly restricted. Only accredited researchers are allowed entry, and even then, they must undergo a rigorous application process and are limited in the number of documents they can view each day. This limited access has led to speculation and conspiracy theories about what might be hidden within the archives. Some believe that the archives contain evidence of secret church doctrines, suppressed texts, or even details about extraterrestrial life. While these theories are largely unfounded, the restricted nature of the archives continues to fuel curiosity and speculation about what secrets they might hold.

In addition to its archives, the Vatican is home to a wealth of artistic and cultural treasures. The Vatican Museums house one of the world's most impressive collections of art, including works by masters such as Michelangelo, Raphael, and Leonardo da Vinci. The Sistine Chapel, with its iconic ceiling painted by Michelangelo, is one of the most famous artistic achievements in history and a testament to the Church's patronage of the arts. These treasures not only reflect the Church's religious significance but also its role as a major cultural and intellectual center throughout history.

The Vatican's influence extends far beyond its religious and cultural contributions. For centuries, the papacy has played a significant role in global politics, often acting as a powerful diplomatic force. The Vatican maintains formal diplomatic relations with over 180 countries and has been involved in numerous international negotiations and peace efforts. The Holy See, the ecclesiastical jurisdiction of the Catholic Church in Rome, is recognized as a sovereign entity in international law, giving it a unique status and influence on the world stage.

Throughout its history, the Vatican has been embroiled in numerous political controversies and power struggles. During the Middle Ages and the Renaissance, the papacy was often a key player in European politics, with popes wielding considerable power over monarchs and states. The infamous Borgia family, which produced two popes, is perhaps the most notorious example of the papacy's involvement in political intrigue. Pope Alexander VI, born Rodrigo Borgia, is often remembered for his ruthless pursuit of power, alleged corruption, and scandalous personal life. His papacy is a reminder of the complex and often controversial role that the Vatican has played in history.

In more recent times, the Vatican has faced its share of scandals and controversies. One of the most significant is the issue of sexual abuse within the Church, which has come to light in the past few decades. Numerous cases of abuse by clergy members have been reported worldwide, leading to widespread outrage and calls for reform. The Vatican has been criticized for its handling of these cases, with allegations of cover-ups and insufficient action to address the problem. Pope Francis, the current head of the Catholic Church, has taken steps to address the issue, including implementing new measures to hold clergy accountable and offering support to victims. However, the scandal continues to cast a shadow over the Church and its leadership.

Another area of controversy is the Vatican's financial dealings. The Vatican's finances are notoriously opaque, with allegations of corruption, mismanagement, and embezzlement frequently making headlines. The Vatican Bank, officially known as the Institute for the Works of Religion, has been at the center of many of these controversies. The bank has faced numerous scandals over the years, including accusations of money laundering and financial impropriety. Efforts to reform the Vatican's financial system have been ongoing, with Pope Francis making significant changes to increase transparency and accountability. However, the issue remains a complex and challenging problem for the Church.

The Vatican's role in international diplomacy is another area of intrigue and secrecy. As a sovereign entity with a unique status in international law, the Holy See often engages in behind-the-scenes diplomacy, acting as a mediator in conflicts and a voice for peace and human rights. The Vatican's diplomatic efforts have been instrumental in resolving various international disputes, including its role in mediating the Beagle Channel conflict between Argentina and Chile in the late 1970s and early 1980s. The Vatican also played a key role in the normalization of relations between the United States and Cuba in 2014, with Pope Francis personally intervening to facilitate dialogue between the two countries.

One of the more enigmatic aspects of the Vatican's influence is its relationship with secret societies and organizations. Throughout history, the Vatican has been linked to various secretive groups, including the Freemasons and the Illuminati. While many of these connections are based on speculation and conspiracy theories, they reflect a broader perception of the Vatican as a center of power and intrigue. The Church's relationship with the Freemasons, for example, has been a subject of controversy for centuries, with the Church officially condemning the organization and its members. Despite this, rumors and theories about secret dealings and alliances continue to circulate, adding to the aura of mystery surrounding the Vatican.

The Vatican is also home to numerous unexplained mysteries and legends. One of the most intriguing is the story of the "Prophecy of the Popes," a series of cryptic predictions attributed to Saint Malachy, a 12th-century Irish bishop. According to the prophecy, there will be a finite number of popes, and the final pope will preside over the end of the world. The prophecy lists a series of mottos or descriptions for each pope, with many interpreting these as predictions of specific events or characteristics of the papal reigns. While the authenticity of the prophecy is widely disputed, it has captured the imagination of many and remains a popular topic of speculation.

Another mysterious aspect of the Vatican is its supposed involvement with extraterrestrial life. Some conspiracy theories suggest that the Vatican holds secret information about the existence of aliens and that it has been involved in covert efforts to communicate with or study extraterrestrial beings. While these theories lack credible evidence, they reflect a broader fascination with the idea that the Vatican might possess hidden knowledge about the universe and humanity's place within it. The Vatican's own interest in astronomy, as evidenced by the Vatican Observatory, one of the oldest astronomical research institutions in the world, adds a layer of intrigue to these theories.

The Vatican's role as the spiritual center of the Catholic Church also involves numerous rituals, ceremonies, and traditions that are steeped in symbolism and secrecy. The election of a new pope, known as the papal conclave, is one of the most closely guarded and secretive processes in the world. The conclave takes place in the Sistine Chapel, where the cardinals of the Church gather to vote in complete seclusion. The process is shrouded in ritual and tradition, with the outcome signaled by the famous white or black smoke rising from the chapel's chimney. The secrecy of the conclave, combined with its ancient rituals, adds to the mystique of the Vatican and the papacy.

The Vatican also plays a central role in the preservation and dissemination of religious knowledge and doctrine. The Congregation for the Doctrine of the Faith, formerly known as the Holy Office, is responsible for safeguarding the teachings of the Church and addressing issues of doctrine and theology. This congregation has a long and controversial history, including its involvement in the Inquisition, during which it sought to root out heresy and enforce orthodoxy within the Church. The legacy of the Inquisition and the Church's efforts to control religious knowledge and belief continue to influence perceptions of the Vatican as a guardian of secret and sometimes controversial doctrines.

Despite its many secrets and controversies, the Vatican remains a place of immense spiritual significance for millions of Catholics around the world. It is a site of pilgrimage, prayer, and worship, where believers come to connect with their faith and seek guidance and inspiration. The Vatican's role as the heart of the Catholic Church, with its rich history and traditions, continues to inspire and influence people across the globe. Its secrets, both real and imagined, add to the allure and mystique of this unique and fascinating institution, ensuring that the Vatican will remain a subject of intrigue and fascination for generations to come.

Chapter 25: The Manchurian Candidate Theory

The Manchurian Candidate Theory, rooted in Cold War anxieties and popularized by Richard Condon's 1959 novel and its subsequent film adaptations, revolves around the concept of brainwashing and psychological manipulation to create unwitting political assassins. The theory posits that individuals can be subjected to such intense psychological conditioning that they can be transformed into obedient automatons, programmed to carry out specific missions against their will or knowledge. This concept plays on deep-seated fears of mind control, espionage, and the erosion of free will, making it a potent subject of fascination and speculation.

The term "Manchurian Candidate" itself has become synonymous with the idea of a sleeper agent, someone who appears normal but has been covertly trained and conditioned to perform acts of sabotage or assassination. The origins of the theory can be traced back to the geopolitical tensions of the mid-20th century, particularly the Korean War, where reports emerged of American prisoners of war being subjected to brutal psychological tactics by their captors. These reports, coupled with the fear of Communist brainwashing techniques, provided fertile ground for the development of the Manchurian Candidate narrative.

In Condon's novel, the protagonist, Raymond Shaw, is a Korean War veteran who is captured by the Chinese and subjected to brainwashing. Upon his return to the United States, Shaw is lauded as a war hero, but unbeknownst to him, he has been conditioned to become an assassin who can be triggered by a specific stimulus, in this case, the sight of a Queen of Diamonds playing card. This narrative device underscores the sinister notion that a seemingly innocuous element can activate a deeply buried, malevolent command within an individual.

The theory taps into the broader anxieties of the era, reflecting the pervasive fear of Communist infiltration and the loss of personal autonomy. The notion that a person could be programmed to act against their own nation, or even their own values, without their conscious awareness, resonated deeply with a public already on edge from the constant threat of nuclear war and the perceived ubiquity of Communist spies. The chilling implications of such a scenario, where the enemy could be anyone, anywhere, at any time, amplified the paranoia and suspicion that characterized the Cold War period.

Scientific advancements in the field of psychology and the understanding of human behavior further fueled these fears. The infamous MKUltra program, conducted by the CIA, sought to explore the possibilities of mind control through various means, including the administration of drugs, hypnosis, and sensory deprivation. While the full extent of the program's success remains shrouded in secrecy, its existence confirmed the government's interest in and willingness to explore the boundaries of human manipulation. The revelations about MKUltra in the 1970s provided a real-world parallel to the fictional Manchurian Candidate, cementing the theory's plausibility in the public consciousness.

The cultural impact of the Manchurian Candidate Theory extends beyond its Cold War origins. It has been referenced and reinterpreted in various forms of media, from films and television shows to literature and political discourse. The theory's enduring appeal lies in its exploration of the dark side of human psychology and the terrifying potential for individuals to be stripped of their agency and used as tools for nefarious purposes. This concept challenges the very notion of identity and autonomy, raising questions about the nature of free will and the extent to which individuals can be influenced or controlled by external forces.

In the realm of political discourse, the term "Manchurian Candidate" is often used to describe politicians or public figures who are perceived to be acting under the influence or control of foreign powers or hidden agendas. This usage underscores the ongoing relevance of the theory, as concerns about foreign interference and the integrity of democratic institutions continue to dominate contemporary political debates. The idea that a seemingly loyal and trustworthy individual could be covertly manipulated to undermine national interests remains a potent and unsettling possibility.

The Manchurian Candidate Theory also intersects with broader themes of conspiracy and mistrust in authority. The notion that shadowy organizations or foreign governments could exert such profound control over individuals feeds into a larger narrative of suspicion and cynicism towards established power structures. This perspective often leads to a questioning of official narratives and a search for hidden truths, reinforcing the idea that reality is not always as it seems and that unseen forces may be at play behind the scenes.

As technology advances and our understanding of the human mind deepens, the Manchurian Candidate Theory continues to evolve, reflecting new anxieties and possibilities. The rise of artificial intelligence and sophisticated surveillance techniques introduces new dimensions to the concept of mind control and manipulation. The potential for digital brainwashing or the use of algorithms to influence behavior and decision-making adds a contemporary twist to the age-old fear of losing control over one's own mind.

Chapter 26: The Hindenburg Disaster Cover-Up

The Hindenburg disaster, which occurred on May 6, 1937, stands as one of the most infamous airship accidents in history. The German passenger airship LZ 129 Hindenburg was attempting to dock with its mooring mast at the Naval Air Station Lakehurst in Manchester Township, New Jersey, when it caught fire and was destroyed. Of the 97 people on board, 36 passengers and crew members perished, along with one worker on the ground. The disaster was a shocking event that marked the end of the airship era and the beginning of extensive speculation and conspiracy theories surrounding the cause of the catastrophe. Central to these theories is the idea of a cover-up, suggesting that the true cause of the disaster was concealed from the public.

The Hindenburg was a marvel of aviation engineering and symbolized German ingenuity and technological prowess. It was the largest airship ever built and was designed for transatlantic flights, offering luxurious accommodations for its passengers. Its maiden flight took place in March 1936, and over the next year, it completed numerous successful voyages between Europe and the Americas. The airship's tragic end, however, overshadowed these accomplishments and left many questions unanswered.

Official investigations into the disaster were conducted by both German and American authorities. The most widely accepted explanation for the fire is that it was caused by a spark that ignited the hydrogen gas used to lift the airship. The exact source of the spark remains a matter of debate, with theories ranging from static electricity to a discharge from the ship's engines. However, the simplicity of this explanation has not satisfied all researchers and enthusiasts, leading to numerous alternative theories and accusations of a cover-up.

One of the most prominent conspiracy theories suggests that the Hindenburg was sabotaged. Proponents of this theory point to the political climate of the time, noting that the airship was a symbol of Nazi Germany and that its destruction could have been an act of anti-Nazi sabotage. Some have speculated that a bomb was planted on the airship, possibly by someone with access to its interior. This theory is supported by reports of suspicious individuals and unexplained events leading up to the disaster, although no concrete evidence has ever been found to substantiate these claims.

Another aspect of the cover-up theory involves the materials used in the construction of the Hindenburg. Critics argue that the airship's skin was coated with highly flammable substances, which could have contributed to the rapid spread of the fire. The official investigations did not place significant emphasis on this possibility, leading some to believe that there was a deliberate attempt to downplay the role of these materials in the disaster. In recent years, scientific tests have suggested that the airship's skin was indeed more flammable than previously acknowledged, lending some credence to this aspect of the cover-up theory.

The involvement of the German government in the investigation has also been a point of contention. At the time of the disaster, Germany was under Nazi rule, and the regime had a vested interest in protecting its reputation and the image of its technological achievements. Some theorists argue that the German authorities may have manipulated the investigation to avoid any findings that could damage the prestige of the Nazi regime or implicate German industry in the disaster. This has led to suspicions that crucial evidence was overlooked or suppressed.

Moreover, the role of the Zeppelin Company, which built and operated the Hindenburg, has come under scrutiny. The company had a strong incentive to preserve its business interests and protect its reputation. In the aftermath of the disaster, the Zeppelin Company was quick to attribute the fire to an accident, dismissing other potential causes. Critics argue that the company's influence over the investigation may have resulted in a biased conclusion that downplayed the possibility of sabotage or material flaws.

The media's portrayal of the disaster has also been a factor in the persistence of cover-up theories. The dramatic and iconic images of the burning airship, along with the famous radio broadcast by Herbert Morrison, who emotionally exclaimed, "Oh, the humanity!" have cemented the Hindenburg disaster in the public consciousness. However, some theorists believe that the media coverage was manipulated to focus on the human tragedy and the supposed accidental nature of the fire, thereby diverting attention from any potential malfeasance.

In the years following the disaster, several individuals and researchers have continued to explore alternative explanations and challenge the official narrative. Books, documentaries, and academic papers have delved into various aspects of the event, from the technical details of the airship's construction to the political context of the time. These efforts have kept the debate alive and ensured that the Hindenburg disaster remains a subject of intrigue and speculation.

One of the more recent theories involves the potential for electrostatic discharge as the trigger for the fire. Some researchers have suggested that the airship's approach to the mooring mast in a stormy atmosphere created conditions ripe for a static discharge. This theory posits that the airship accumulated a static charge as it passed through the atmosphere and that this charge was released when the ship neared the mast, igniting the hydrogen. This explanation attempts to bridge the gap between the official spark theory and the alternative sabotage and material flaw theories, providing a more nuanced understanding of the disaster.

Despite the numerous theories and investigations, the true cause of the Hindenburg disaster remains elusive. The complexity of the event, coupled with the limitations of the technology and investigative methods of the time, means that a definitive answer may never be found. However, the persistence of cover-up theories highlights the enduring fascination with the disaster and the human need to seek answers and assign meaning to tragic events.

Chapter 27: The Ghosts of the White House

The White House, the official residence and workplace of the President of the United States, is one of the most famous buildings in the world. Its storied halls have seen momentous events in American history, from historic legislative decisions to dramatic personal moments of its occupants. But beyond its political significance, the White House is also renowned for its rich history of ghostly encounters and supernatural phenomena. Stories of spectral sightings and unexplained occurrences have been part of the mansion's lore for centuries, contributing to the legend of the "Ghosts of the White House."

The most frequently reported apparition is that of Abraham Lincoln, the 16th President of the United States. Lincoln's tragic assassination in 1865 left an indelible mark on the nation's history, and his ghost is said to linger in the White House, particularly in the Lincoln Bedroom. Numerous accounts from staff, visitors, and even other presidents have described encounters with Lincoln's spectral figure. One of the most famous reports comes from First Lady Eleanor Roosevelt, who felt Lincoln's presence while working in the Lincoln Bedroom. British Prime Minister Winston Churchill also claimed to have seen Lincoln's ghost while staying at the White House during World War II. Churchill's encounter was particularly striking; he reported seeing Lincoln by the fireplace, a sight that so startled him that he refused to stay in the room again.

Other spirits said to haunt the White House include First Lady Abigail Adams, who lived in the mansion during its early years. She was known for hanging laundry in the East Room, and there have been numerous reports of her ghost, often described as a figure in a lace shawl, appearing in that area. Staff and visitors have claimed to see her ghostly figure carrying a laundry basket, her presence often accompanied by the faint scent of lavender.

Dolly Madison, another former First Lady, is believed to haunt the Rose Garden. Madison was instrumental in planning and planting the original garden, and it is said that when gardeners attempted to alter the garden's layout during the Wilson administration, Madison's ghost appeared to stop them. Frightened by her apparition, the gardeners reportedly abandoned their plans, and the Rose Garden was left unchanged.

President Andrew Jackson is another spirit said to haunt the White House. His ghost is believed to linger in the Rose Room, which was his bedroom during his presidency. Various accounts describe hearing Jackson's hearty laughter and angry stomping in the room. Mary Todd Lincoln, who held séances in the White House after her son Willie's death, also reported feeling Jackson's presence. The Rose Room has since become known as one of the most haunted rooms in the mansion.

The ghost of Willie Lincoln, President Lincoln's young son who died of typhoid fever in the White House in 1862, is also said to make appearances. Willie's death deeply affected his parents, and his spirit is believed to linger in the White House. There have been reports of his ghost playing in the hallways, and several staff members have claimed to hear the sound of a child running and laughing.

Another notable apparition is that of David Burns, the original owner of the land where the White House now stands. Burns was a wealthy plantation owner who reluctantly sold his land to the government. His spirit has been seen and heard in various parts of the mansion, often identified by his distinctive voice. In one account, a guard reported hearing a voice saying, "I am Mr. Burns," echoing through the hallways.

The White House has also been linked to more recent spectral sightings. President Harry S. Truman once wrote to his wife about being awakened by knocks on his bedroom door, only to find no one there. He described hearing footsteps in the hall and the sensation of being watched, leading him to believe the building was haunted. President Ronald Reagan and his daughter Maureen also reported strange occurrences. Reagan's dog, Rex, would often bark frantically at the entrance to the Lincoln Bedroom and refuse to enter.

Despite the numerous reports of ghostly encounters, the White House remains a place of great historical and cultural significance. Its haunted reputation adds an intriguing layer to its storied past, blending history and legend in a unique way. The idea that the spirits of former residents and visitors might still roam its halls speaks to the powerful emotions and momentous events that have transpired within its walls. Whether or not one believes in ghosts, the tales of the White House's spectral inhabitants provide a fascinating glimpse into the personal lives and enduring legacies of those who have shaped American history.

The accounts of hauntings at the White House have been the subject of various books, documentaries, and tours, further cementing the mansion's reputation as one of the most haunted places in the United States. Ghost hunters and paranormal enthusiasts often regard the White House as a prime location for supernatural activity, and its ghost stories continue to captivate the public's imagination. These tales offer a compelling narrative that complements the historical significance of the building, providing a deeper, more personal connection to the past.

In addition to the well-known ghosts, there are numerous lesser-known apparitions and unexplained phenomena reported at the White House. For instance, during the Taft administration, staff members reported seeing the ghost of a young boy known as "The Thing." This spirit was said to appear as a small figure and was believed to be the ghost of a servant or a child who once lived on the premises. The sightings of "The Thing" were so frequent that President William Howard Taft ordered an investigation, but no conclusive explanation was ever found.

Another mysterious presence is that of an unidentified British soldier, believed to have died during the War of 1812. This ghost is often seen near the North Portico and is said to be a remnant of the time when British troops set fire to the White House. The soldier's forlorn figure has been described by various witnesses, adding another layer to the rich tapestry of ghostly lore associated with the mansion.

The ghost of Anna Surratt, daughter of Mary Surratt, one of the conspirators in the assassination of President Lincoln, is also said to haunt the White House. Anna's spirit is believed to appear at the North Entrance, pleading for her mother's life. Mary Surratt was the first woman executed by the federal government, and Anna's ghostly presence is thought to be a manifestation of her desperate attempts to save her mother.

The White House also has its share of poltergeist activity, with reports of doors slamming, lights flickering, and unexplained cold spots throughout the building. These occurrences are often attributed to the restless spirits of past inhabitants and have been documented by various staff members and residents over the years. The combination of residual energy from historical events and the emotional intensity of the lives lived within the mansion's walls create an environment ripe for paranormal activity.

While the stories of the White House's ghosts are fascinating, they also serve as a reminder of the human element behind historical events. The apparitions of former presidents, first ladies, and other figures connect us to the personal struggles, triumphs, and tragedies that have shaped the course of American history. The ghostly legends of the White House provide a unique perspective on the lives of those who have inhabited the mansion, offering a glimpse into the emotional and psychological impact of their experiences.

In exploring the ghostly history of the White House, one also encounters the broader cultural significance of ghost stories in American society. These tales reflect a deep-seated fascination with the unknown and the afterlife, as well as a desire to connect with the past in a tangible way. The ghost stories of the White House are not just about spectral sightings; they are about the enduring presence of history and the ways in which it continues to shape our understanding of the present.

Chapter 28: The Montauk Project

The Montauk Project is one of the most enigmatic and controversial conspiracy theories of the late 20th century. Rooted in the Cold War era, the narrative intertwines elements of time travel, mind control, extraterrestrial encounters, and secret government experiments. This intricate web of conspiracies centers around the Montauk Air Force Station, a decommissioned military base located at the eastern tip of Long Island, New York. According to proponents of the Montauk Project theory, this site was the epicenter of clandestine and ethically dubious experiments conducted by the U.S. government, involving everything from psychological warfare to time travel and interdimensional portals.

The origins of the Montauk Project theory are closely linked to the Philadelphia Experiment, another famous conspiracy theory. The Philadelphia Experiment alleges that in 1943, the U.S. Navy attempted to render the USS Eldridge, a destroyer escort, invisible to radar. The experiment supposedly resulted in the ship temporarily disappearing from the Philadelphia Naval Shipyard and reappearing in Norfolk, Virginia. During this process, crew members allegedly suffered from severe physical and psychological trauma, including reports of some being fused into the ship's hull. While the official stance is that the Philadelphia Experiment is a hoax, it serves as the foundational myth for the Montauk Project.

The story of the Montauk Project began to gain traction in the 1980s, primarily through the accounts of Preston B. Nichols and Peter Moon, who co-authored several books on the subject. Nichols, who claimed to have recovered repressed memories of his involvement in the project, detailed his experiences in "The Montauk Project: Experiments in Time," published in 1992. According to Nichols, the Montauk Project evolved from the Philadelphia Experiment's research, aiming to exploit and further develop the science of manipulating space and time.

Nichols' account describes how the project used a massive radar dish at the Montauk Air Force Station to conduct mind control experiments on unwitting subjects. These experiments purportedly involved manipulating human thoughts, inducing amnesia, and creating sleeper agents. The radar dish, a key component of the project, was allegedly capable of transmitting powerful electromagnetic signals that could influence the human mind. This technology was said to be an extension of the mind control research conducted by the CIA under programs like MKUltra, which sought to explore the limits of psychological manipulation through various means, including the use of drugs, hypnosis, and sensory deprivation.

One of the most sensational claims associated with the Montauk Project is the alleged development of time travel technology. Nichols and others have described how the project supposedly created a "time tunnel," a portal that allowed travel to different periods and dimensions. These time tunnels were used for various purposes, including exploring alternate realities, retrieving historical artifacts, and even influencing events in the past and future. The accounts include vivid descriptions of missions to ancient Egypt, Mars, and other fantastical locations.

A central figure in the Montauk Project narrative is a man named Al Bielek. Bielek claimed to have been part of the Philadelphia Experiment and later involved in the Montauk Project. According to his testimony, he and his brother, Duncan Cameron, were transported through time during the Philadelphia Experiment and subsequently participated in experiments at Montauk. Bielek's accounts include detailed descriptions of time travel missions, interactions with extraterrestrial beings, and encounters with advanced technologies. His stories, although widely regarded as far-fetched, have become integral to the lore of the Montauk Project.

The alleged experiments at Montauk also included efforts to create and control psychic abilities. Nichols and others have claimed that the project sought to harness and amplify psychic powers, using subjects with latent abilities to conduct remote viewing, telekinesis, and other paranormal feats. The experiments reportedly involved isolating these individuals in sensory deprivation tanks and subjecting them to intense electromagnetic fields to enhance their psychic capabilities. One particularly famous subject, known only as "The Montauk Boy," was said to possess extraordinary psychic powers that were exploited for various covert operations.

The Montauk Project's connection to extraterrestrial beings is another key element of the conspiracy theory. Proponents assert that the project involved interactions with alien civilizations, who provided advanced technology and knowledge in exchange for human subjects and other resources. These accounts often describe joint human-alien efforts to develop interdimensional travel and other cutting-edge technologies. Some theories even suggest that the Montauk Air Force Station served as a hub for extraterrestrial activity, with underground facilities housing alien spacecraft and research labs.

The Montauk Project also delves into the concept of "reality engineering," where the project's scientists allegedly attempted to manipulate and reshape reality itself. This aspect of the theory posits that the project's ultimate goal was to control human perception and influence events on a global scale. Through a combination of time travel, mind control, and advanced technology, the project aimed to create a malleable reality that could be altered to suit the needs of those in power.

The supposed culmination of the Montauk Project occurred on August 12, 1983, when an experiment allegedly went disastrously wrong. According to Nichols and Bielek, a time portal accidentally connected the Montauk base to the USS Eldridge during the Philadelphia Experiment, creating a rift in the space-time continuum.

This event, known as the "Montauk Chair Incident," supposedly unleashed a monstrous creature from another dimension, which rampaged through the base before being subdued. The incident led to the shutdown of the project and the abandonment of the Montauk Air Force Station.

Despite the sensational nature of these claims, the Montauk Project theory has been met with widespread skepticism. Critics argue that the lack of concrete evidence, the fantastical elements of the story, and the reliance on anecdotal accounts undermine its credibility. Many of the key figures involved, including Nichols and Bielek, have been accused of fabricating their stories or suffering from delusions. Additionally, there is no verifiable documentation or physical evidence to support the existence of the project or its purported experiments.

Nevertheless, the Montauk Project has had a significant impact on popular culture, inspiring books, movies, and television shows. The Netflix series "Stranger Things," for example, draws heavily on the themes and concepts of the Montauk Project, featuring government experiments, interdimensional portals, and psychic children. The series' original working title was even "Montauk," underscoring the direct influence of the conspiracy theory on its storyline.

Chapter 29: The Death of Bruce Lee

The death of Bruce Lee on July 20, 1973, remains one of the most shocking and controversial events in the history of Hollywood and martial arts. Bruce Lee, often hailed as the greatest martial artist of all time, was a charismatic actor, director, and philosopher who revolutionized martial arts cinema and brought Chinese martial arts to the global stage. His sudden death at the age of 32 stunned the world and gave rise to numerous conspiracy theories and speculations that continue to intrigue fans and scholars alike.

Bruce Lee was at the peak of his career in 1973. He had already made a significant impact with his groundbreaking films, such as "The Big Boss," "Fist of Fury," and "Way of the Dragon." His final film, "Enter the Dragon," was poised to cement his status as an international superstar. The film was a joint American and Hong Kong production and marked Lee's first major role in a Hollywood film. It showcased his exceptional martial arts skills and his unique philosophy, blending Eastern and Western cultural elements in a way that resonated with a global audience. Tragically, Lee did not live to see the release of "Enter the Dragon," which premiered just six days after his death.

On the day of his death, Bruce Lee was in Hong Kong, working on the pre-production of his next film, "Game of Death." He spent the afternoon meeting with producers and discussing the film's script. Later, he visited the home of Taiwanese actress Betty Ting Pei, with whom he was working on the project. According to Ting Pei, Lee complained of a headache, and she gave him a painkiller called Equagesic, a combination of aspirin and the tranquilizer meprobamate. After taking the medication, Lee lay down for a nap and never woke up. When attempts to revive him failed, he was rushed to Queen Elizabeth Hospital, where he was pronounced dead on arrival.

The official cause of death was given as cerebral edema, or swelling of the brain. An autopsy revealed that his brain had swollen considerably, from 1,400 to 1,575 grams. The medical examiner attributed the edema to an adverse reaction to the Equagesic. However, the precise cause of Lee's death has been the subject of intense debate and speculation for decades.

One of the most popular theories is that Bruce Lee was the victim of foul play. Some believe that he was poisoned, either intentionally or accidentally, by someone close to him. This theory is fueled by the fact that Lee had been outspoken about his disdain for certain powerful figures in the Hong Kong film industry and the Chinese martial arts community. Lee's meteoric rise and his efforts to break down racial barriers in Hollywood may have also earned him enemies who resented his success and influence.

Another theory suggests that Lee's death was the result of a curse. This idea gained traction in part because of the eerie parallels between Lee's death and that of his son, Brandon Lee, who died under similarly mysterious circumstances nearly 20 years later. Brandon Lee was killed in a tragic accident on the set of the film "The Crow" in 1993, when a prop gun discharged a live round. The notion of a family curse has captivated the public imagination and added a layer of mystique to the Lee family's legacy.

Some have speculated that Bruce Lee's intense physical regimen and the use of performance-enhancing drugs contributed to his death. Lee was known for his rigorous training routines and his dedication to maintaining peak physical condition. He experimented with various supplements and medications to enhance his performance and speed up recovery. There are claims that he may have taken substances that led to a fatal reaction, especially given his history of suffering from severe allergic reactions. In May 1973, just two months before his death, Lee collapsed during an ADR session for "Enter the Dragon" and was diagnosed with cerebral edema, which was successfully treated. This incident suggests that Lee may have been predisposed to such medical emergencies.

Another angle involves the possibility of heatstroke. On the day of his death, Hong Kong was experiencing exceptionally high temperatures, and Lee had spent several hours in a hot room without air conditioning. Lee's body fat percentage was extremely low due to his intense fitness regimen, which some medical experts believe could have made him more susceptible to heatstroke. Heatstroke can cause cerebral edema, the condition that ultimately killed him. This theory is supported by the fact that Lee had his sweat glands surgically removed from his armpits to prevent visible sweating on camera, which may have impaired his body's ability to regulate temperature.

Some conspiracy theorists even suggest that Bruce Lee was assassinated by the Chinese mafia or a rival martial arts faction. According to this theory, Lee's revolutionary ideas and his efforts to share Chinese martial arts with the world angered traditionalists who felt he was betraying their secrets. This factionalism within the martial arts community could have led to a targeted attack on Lee. However, there is little concrete evidence to support this claim, and it remains largely speculative.

In addition to these theories, there are numerous other explanations that have been proposed over the years. Some have suggested that Lee suffered from an undiagnosed medical condition, such as epilepsy or a brain aneurysm. Others believe that the combination of stress, overwork, and his strict dietary regimen may have contributed to his untimely death.

Despite the various theories and the enduring mystery surrounding Bruce Lee's death, the official cause remains an allergic reaction to Equagesic, leading to cerebral edema. This explanation is accepted by most medical professionals, but the lack of definitive evidence and the presence of so many unanswered questions have kept the conspiracy theories alive.

The impact of Bruce Lee's death on popular culture and the martial arts community cannot be overstated. He was more than just a martial artist and actor; he was a cultural icon and a symbol of strength, resilience, and the blending of Eastern and Western philosophies. His films continue to inspire generations of martial artists and actors, and his teachings on martial arts, self-expression, and personal development are studied and revered worldwide.

Bruce Lee's legacy is also preserved through his writings and philosophy. He developed a martial arts philosophy called Jeet Kune Do, which emphasizes adaptability, efficiency, and directness. Jeet Kune Do is not just a fighting style but a way of life, encouraging practitioners to absorb what is useful and reject what is not. This philosophy has influenced countless martial artists and thinkers, and it remains a central part of Lee's enduring influence.

In the years following his death, numerous documentaries, books, and films have been produced to explore Bruce Lee's life, career, and the mystery of his death. His story has been the subject of intense scrutiny and analysis, and his persona has taken on an almost mythic quality. Despite the controversies and conspiracy theories, Bruce Lee's contributions to martial arts and popular culture are undeniable.

In recent years, there has been renewed interest in Bruce Lee's life and legacy, spurred by new biographical works and retrospectives. The 2020 ESPN documentary "Be Water" provides an in-depth look at Lee's life, career, and the challenges he faced as an Asian-American in Hollywood. This documentary highlights Lee's struggles against racial discrimination and his efforts to change the perception of Asian characters in American cinema.

Bruce Lee's influence extends beyond martial arts and cinema. He has become a symbol of Asian-American pride and a pioneer in the fight for racial equality and representation in the media. His efforts to bridge cultural divides and promote understanding between East and West continue to resonate today, making him a timeless figure in the annals of global culture.

Chapter 30: The Chernobyl Disaster Conspiracy

The Chernobyl disaster, which occurred on April 26, 1986, is one of the most catastrophic nuclear accidents in history. The explosion and subsequent fire at the Chernobyl Nuclear Power Plant's Reactor No. 4 in Pripyat, Ukraine, released massive amounts of radioactive particles into the atmosphere. The disaster had far-reaching environmental, health, and political consequences, leading to the evacuation and long-term exclusion of a large area around the plant. While the official narrative attributes the disaster to a combination of reactor design flaws and operator error, numerous conspiracy theories have emerged over the years, suggesting alternative explanations and hidden agendas behind the catastrophe.

One of the primary conspiracy theories surrounding the Chernobyl disaster is the notion that it was a deliberate act of sabotage by the United States or Western intelligence agencies. Proponents of this theory argue that the explosion was orchestrated as part of a Cold War strategy to weaken the Soviet Union economically and politically. The disaster, they claim, was intended to expose the weaknesses of the Soviet nuclear program and undermine public confidence in the government. This theory posits that Western agents infiltrated the plant and tampered with the reactor to induce the explosion. Supporters of this idea often point to the timing of the disaster, occurring at a moment when the Soviet Union was already facing significant economic and political challenges.

Another conspiracy theory suggests that the Chernobyl disaster was a cover-up for a secret weapons program. According to this theory, the Chernobyl plant was not merely a civilian nuclear power station but was also involved in the production of plutonium for nuclear weapons. The explosion, therefore, was not an accident but the result of an experiment or test gone wrong. Advocates of this theory argue that the Soviet authorities used the disaster narrative to hide the true purpose of the facility and to divert attention from their covert military activities. They cite the presence of high-ranking military personnel and the immediate mobilization of the Soviet army in the aftermath of the explosion as evidence of the plant's dual-use nature.

A related theory posits that the Chernobyl disaster was the result of an extraterrestrial intervention. This idea stems from reports of unidentified flying objects (UFOs) being sighted in the vicinity of the plant before and after the explosion. Some witnesses claimed to have seen strange lights and objects hovering over the reactor, leading to speculation that aliens might have been involved in either causing the disaster or mitigating its effects. According to this theory, extraterrestrial beings were monitoring human nuclear activities and intervened to prevent an even greater catastrophe. While this theory lacks substantial evidence, it remains popular among UFO enthusiasts and conspiracy theorists.

Another angle of the Chernobyl conspiracy theories involves internal sabotage by dissident elements within the Soviet government or military. This theory suggests that the disaster was orchestrated by factions opposed to Mikhail Gorbachev's policies of glasnost (openness) and perestroika (restructuring). By causing a major disaster, these elements hoped to destabilize Gorbachev's administration and derail his reforms. Supporters of this theory argue that the timing of the disaster, during a period of significant political change, and the subsequent handling of the crisis by Soviet authorities point to deliberate sabotage rather than mere incompetence.

Additionally, some theories propose that the Chernobyl disaster was an experiment in psychological warfare. According to this idea, the Soviet government used the disaster as a means to study the effects of extreme stress and trauma on the population. By observing the reactions of the evacuated residents and the emergency responders, the authorities could gather valuable data on human behavior under crisis conditions. This theory suggests that the disaster was a controlled event, designed to produce specific psychological outcomes. Proponents of this idea often point to the extensive monitoring and documentation of the disaster's aftermath as evidence of an underlying experimental agenda.

One of the more plausible conspiracy theories involves the cover-up and mismanagement by Soviet authorities. It is well-documented that the Soviet government initially downplayed the severity of the disaster, delaying the evacuation of Pripyat and failing to provide adequate information to the public and the international community. Some conspiracy theorists argue that this cover-up was part of a broader strategy to protect the Soviet nuclear industry and avoid political fallout. They suggest that the authorities knew the reactor design was flawed and that safety protocols were inadequate, but chose to ignore these issues to maintain the image of Soviet technological superiority. This theory is supported by the numerous reports of suppressed information, doctored records, and the persecution of whistleblowers in the aftermath of the disaster.

Another conspiracy theory centers on the alleged presence of a mysterious device known as the "Chernobyl-2" or "Duga" radar system, located near the Chernobyl plant. The Duga radar, part of the Soviet missile defense early-warning system, was known for its distinctive "Woodpecker" signal heard on shortwave radio frequencies. Some theorists believe that the radar system played a role in the disaster, either through electromagnetic interference with the reactor's control systems or as part of a secret experiment. They argue that the proximity of the Duga radar to the Chernobyl plant is too coincidental to be ignored and suggest that the disaster may have been linked to covert military operations involving the radar.

The theory of a Soviet cover-up is further supported by the accounts of individuals like Valery Legasov, a prominent Soviet chemist who was part of the investigation into the Chernobyl disaster. Legasov's posthumously released tapes revealed his frustrations with the Soviet bureaucracy and its attempts to suppress information about the true causes of the disaster. His testimony highlighted the systemic issues within the Soviet nuclear industry, including poor safety standards, lack of transparency, and the prioritization of political considerations over public safety. These revelations lend credence to the idea that the disaster was not merely an accident but the result of a deeply flawed system.

Another aspect of the Chernobyl conspiracy theories involves the long-term health effects of radiation exposure. Some theorists claim that the true extent of the health impacts has been deliberately concealed by governments and international organizations. They argue that the official figures on cancer rates, birth defects, and other radiation-related illnesses are significantly understated and that the full scale of the disaster's consequences has been hidden to avoid public panic and liability. This theory is supported by the discrepancies in health data and the ongoing debates among scientists and researchers about the long-term effects of low-level radiation exposure.

In addition to these conspiracy theories, the Chernobyl disaster has also inspired a range of speculative fiction and popular culture narratives. The 2019 HBO miniseries "Chernobyl," for example, dramatizes the events of the disaster and explores the themes of government cover-ups, human error, and the consequences of technological hubris. While the series is based on historical events, it has also contributed to the public's fascination with the disaster and the various conspiracy theories surrounding it. The show emphasizes the heroism of the first responders and the tragic consequences of the disaster, while also highlighting the systemic failures and the culture of secrecy within the Soviet Union.

The legacy of the Chernobyl disaster continues to resonate today, both in the ongoing environmental and health impacts and in the cultural memory of the event. The Chernobyl Exclusion Zone has become a site of dark tourism, attracting visitors from around the world who are fascinated by the abandoned city of Pripyat and the remnants of the disaster. This interest in Chernobyl reflects a broader cultural fascination with nuclear disasters and the apocalyptic imagery they evoke.

Chapter 31: The Lindbergh Baby Kidnapping

The Lindbergh baby kidnapping, one of the most notorious crimes of the 20th century, captivated the world with its dramatic twists and unsolved mysteries. On the night of March 1, 1932, Charles Augustus Lindbergh Jr., the 20-month-old son of famous aviator Charles Lindbergh and his wife, Anne Morrow Lindbergh, was abducted from his crib in the family's secluded home in Hopewell, New Jersey. The kidnapping set off a nationwide manhunt and became a major media sensation, leading to widespread public speculation and numerous conspiracy theories.

The Lindberghs had put their son to bed around 8:00 PM, and the child's nurse, Betty Gow, checked on him at 9:00 PM. When Gow returned around 10:00 PM, she found the crib empty. A ransom note demanding $50,000 was discovered on the nursery windowsill. The note was crudely written and full of grammatical errors, indicating that the kidnappers were not highly educated. It instructed the Lindberghs to expect further communication and warned against contacting the police, though the Lindberghs did so immediately.

The investigation was initially led by the New Jersey State Police, with Colonel H. Norman Schwarzkopf, father of the future General H. Norman Schwarzkopf Jr., at the helm. The FBI, then a fledgling organization under J. Edgar Hoover, also became involved. The case drew significant media attention, with journalists and the public closely following every development. The Lindberghs were inundated with letters from well-wishers, psychics, and cranks, offering tips and demanding rewards.

The kidnappers sent several more ransom notes over the following weeks, increasing the ransom to $70,000. These notes were delivered through various intermediaries, including a retired teacher named Dr.

John F. Condon, who volunteered to act as a go-between. Using the pseudonym "Jafsie," Condon placed ads in the newspapers, communicating with the kidnappers and negotiating the terms of the ransom. The ordeal included several false leads and misdirections, adding to the confusion and desperation of the Lindbergh family and the authorities.

On April 2, 1932, Condon met with a man calling himself "John" in a Bronx cemetery. After an exchange of coded messages and much negotiation, Condon handed over the ransom money, which was paid in gold certificates—a detail that would later become crucial in the investigation. In return, "John" gave Condon a note indicating the location of the kidnapped child. However, when authorities searched the specified location, they found no sign of the baby.

The breakthrough in the case came on May 12, 1932, when the decomposed body of a small child was discovered by a truck driver named William Allen, about four miles from the Lindbergh home. The child had been dead for some time and was partially buried in a shallow grave. Despite the advanced state of decomposition, the body was positively identified as that of Charles Lindbergh Jr. The discovery of the child's body led to widespread public mourning and a renewed determination to catch the perpetrators.

The investigation into the kidnapping and murder continued, with authorities meticulously tracing the ransom money. The breakthrough came in September 1934, when a $10 gold certificate from the ransom was used to purchase gasoline in New York City. The attendant noted the license plate number of the car, which led police to Bruno Richard Hauptmann, a German immigrant and carpenter living in the Bronx.

Hauptmann was arrested on September 19, 1934. A search of his home uncovered $14,600 of the ransom money hidden in his garage, as well as other incriminating evidence, including Condon's phone number and address. Hauptmann denied any involvement in the kidnapping, claiming that the money had been left with him by a former business associate named Isidor Fisch, who had since died. Despite his protests, Hauptmann was charged with the kidnapping and murder of Charles Lindbergh Jr.

The trial, held in Flemington, New Jersey, in January 1935, was a media circus, drawing immense public interest and coverage. Dubbed the "Trial of the Century," it featured dramatic testimonies, intense cross-examinations, and a public eager for justice. The prosecution, led by Attorney General David T. Wilentz, presented a strong case against Hauptmann, including the ransom money found in his possession, handwriting analysis linking him to the ransom notes, and witness testimonies placing him near the Lindbergh home on the night of the kidnapping.

Hauptmann's defense, led by Edward J. Reilly, argued that Hauptmann was innocent and had been framed. They maintained that the ransom money had indeed been left with Hauptmann by Isidor Fisch and that Hauptmann had no knowledge of its origins. They also pointed to the lack of direct evidence linking Hauptmann to the crime scene and questioned the reliability of the handwriting analysis.

Despite the defense's efforts, the jury found Hauptmann guilty of first-degree murder on February 13, 1935. He was sentenced to death and was executed in the electric chair at the New Jersey State Prison on April 3, 1936. Hauptmann continued to profess his innocence until the end, and his conviction did not put an end to the speculation and conspiracy theories surrounding the case.

One of the most persistent conspiracy theories suggests that Hauptmann was innocent and that the true perpetrators were never caught. Some believe that Hauptmann was a convenient scapegoat for a bungled investigation and that the real kidnappers were either protected by influential connections or had covered their tracks too well. This theory is fueled by inconsistencies in the evidence and the possibility that the police planted the ransom money in Hauptmann's garage to secure a conviction.

Another theory posits that the kidnapping was an inside job, orchestrated by someone close to the Lindbergh family. Speculation has centered on Betty Gow, the child's nurse, and other household staff. Proponents of this theory argue that the kidnapper's detailed knowledge of the Lindbergh home and the precise timing of the abduction suggest an insider's involvement. Some even suggest that the Lindberghs themselves may have been complicit, although this theory is widely dismissed due to a lack of credible evidence.

There are also theories that point to organized crime involvement. During the Prohibition era, organized crime syndicates were powerful and well-connected, and some suggest that they orchestrated the kidnapping for financial gain or as leverage against the Lindbergh family. This theory is supported by the fact that several individuals with ties to organized crime were investigated during the case, although no conclusive evidence was found to link them to the kidnapping.

In addition to these theories, there are numerous other speculations about the Lindbergh baby kidnapping, ranging from the involvement of rogue law enforcement officers to elaborate plots involving foreign espionage. Each theory reflects the complex social and political landscape of the time, as well as the enduring fascination with one of the most high-profile crimes in American history.

The Lindbergh baby kidnapping had far-reaching consequences beyond the immediate tragedy. The case led to significant changes in law enforcement and criminal justice in the United States. One of the most notable outcomes was the passage of the Federal Kidnapping Act, also known as the "Lindbergh Law," in 1932. This law made kidnapping a federal offense, allowing the FBI to take a more active role in investigating such crimes and providing greater resources for pursuing kidnappers across state lines.

The case also had a profound impact on the Lindbergh family. Charles and Anne Lindbergh retreated from the public eye, seeking privacy and security after the intense media scrutiny and personal trauma. They had five more children after Charles Jr.'s death and eventually moved to Europe in an attempt to escape the public attention. Charles Lindbergh continued his aviation career and became an advocate for various causes, but the shadow of the kidnapping and its aftermath lingered throughout his life.

The Lindbergh baby kidnapping remains a subject of ongoing fascination and debate. The case has inspired numerous books, films, and documentaries, each exploring different aspects of the crime and its investigation. It stands as a stark reminder of the vulnerabilities and complexities of the human experience, illustrating how a single event can ripple through history, shaping laws, lives, and collective memory.

Chapter 32: The Pearl Harbor Attack Forewarning

The attack on Pearl Harbor on December 7, 1941, stands as one of the most significant and devastating events in American history. It led to the United States' entry into World War II and changed the course of the war. However, the attack also sparked numerous conspiracy theories and controversies, primarily centered around the idea that the United States had forewarning of the attack and either failed to act or intentionally allowed it to happen for strategic reasons. These theories have fueled decades of debate among historians, military analysts, and the public, seeking to understand the extent to which the U.S. government might have known about the impending attack and why such knowledge, if it existed, did not prevent the catastrophe.

The official narrative holds that the attack on Pearl Harbor by the Imperial Japanese Navy was a surprise, catching the U.S. Pacific Fleet and its personnel off guard. The attack resulted in the loss of over 2,400 American lives, the destruction of numerous ships and aircraft, and significant damage to the naval base. In the immediate aftermath, President Franklin D. Roosevelt described the day as "a date which will live in infamy," and Congress declared war on Japan, bringing the United States fully into World War II.

However, some historians and conspiracy theorists argue that the U.S. government, and specifically key figures within it, had prior knowledge of Japan's plans to attack Pearl Harbor. This theory is often referred to as the "forewarning" or "advance-knowledge" theory. Proponents of this theory point to several pieces of evidence that suggest the possibility of forewarning, including intercepted Japanese communications, diplomatic warnings, and the movements and decisions of key military personnel.

One of the central pieces of evidence cited by proponents of the forewarning theory is the series of intercepted Japanese communications, often referred to as "Magic" intercepts. "Magic" was the codename for the U.S. efforts to decrypt Japanese diplomatic and military communications. By late 1940 and early 1941, American cryptanalysts had made significant progress in breaking Japan's codes, providing valuable intelligence on Japanese intentions and operations. Critics argue that these intercepts contained clues about Japan's plans to attack Pearl Harbor, but that the information was either not properly analyzed or was deliberately ignored by those in power.

For example, one significant intercept, often cited by proponents of the theory, is a message from Japanese Foreign Minister Shigenori Togo to the Japanese ambassador in Washington, Kichisaburo Nomura, in which Togo outlined Japan's plan to sever diplomatic relations with the United States if negotiations failed. This message, intercepted on November 19, 1941, suggested that Japan was preparing for a drastic action, which some interpret as an indication of the impending attack on Pearl Harbor. However, defenders of the official narrative argue that while the message indicated a breakdown in diplomacy, it did not provide specific details about the attack on Pearl Harbor.

Another piece of evidence often highlighted by conspiracy theorists is the so-called "Winds Code" messages. In late November 1941, Japanese diplomats received instructions on how to use coded phrases in weather broadcasts to signal the breakdown of negotiations and the onset of war. The phrase "east wind, rain" was to signal a break with the United States. On December 4, 1941, American monitoring stations picked up what some believe was the "east wind, rain" message. However, the significance of this message remains debated, as there is no clear consensus on whether it was indeed the warning signal or whether it was properly understood by American analysts.

Diplomatic warnings from foreign governments also play a crucial role in the forewarning theory. In the months leading up to the attack, several governments, including those of the Netherlands, Britain, and the Soviet Union, allegedly provided the United States with intelligence suggesting that Japan was planning a major offensive in the Pacific. One particularly controversial claim involves a supposed warning from the Soviet Union, based on intelligence from the Sorge spy ring in Tokyo, which allegedly informed the United States of Japan's plans to attack Pearl Harbor. However, the veracity and impact of these warnings are difficult to ascertain, as much of the documentation remains classified or has been lost over time.

Additionally, some conspiracy theorists point to the movements and decisions of key military personnel as evidence of forewarning. They argue that the U.S. commanders at Pearl Harbor, Admiral Husband E. Kimmel and General Walter C. Short, were not adequately informed about the intelligence indicating a potential attack. Critics suggest that high-ranking officials in Washington, including President Roosevelt, deliberately withheld this information to ensure that the attack would proceed, thereby galvanizing American public opinion and providing a pretext for entering the war. This theory is often referred to as the "back door to war" theory.

One notable aspect of this theory involves the decision to send the aircraft carriers, USS Enterprise and USS Lexington, on missions away from Pearl Harbor in the days leading up to the attack. Conspiracy theorists argue that this move, combined with the dispersal of other key ships and the lack of a heightened alert status, suggests that some officials knew about the impending attack and took steps to protect vital assets while leaving the base vulnerable enough to ensure a dramatic and galvanizing event.

The "back door to war" theory also posits that Roosevelt and his advisors believed that entering World War II was essential for both strategic and economic reasons. The U.S. was already providing significant support to the Allies through programs like Lend-Lease, and there was a growing recognition that a German victory in Europe and Japanese dominance in the Pacific would threaten American interests. According to this theory, allowing the Pearl Harbor attack to happen was a calculated risk to unify the American public and overcome isolationist sentiment.

Critics of the forewarning theory argue that it is based on selective interpretation of evidence and hindsight bias. They maintain that while there were indeed signals and warnings of an impending Japanese offensive, these were often vague, contradictory, and did not specifically indicate an attack on Pearl Harbor. Intelligence agencies at the time were overwhelmed with information, much of which was ambiguous and required careful analysis. The chaotic nature of intelligence work, combined with interagency rivalries and communication breakdowns, contributed to the failure to piece together the complete picture.

Moreover, defenders of the official narrative emphasize that the U.S. military and government did take some steps to prepare for a potential conflict with Japan. For instance, the Pacific Fleet had been relocated from its base in San Diego to Pearl Harbor in 1940 as a deterrent measure. Additionally, there were efforts to fortify American positions in the Pacific, although these measures were hampered by resource limitations and bureaucratic inertia.

The debate over whether the U.S. had forewarning of the Pearl Harbor attack also delves into broader issues of historical interpretation and the nature of conspiracy theories. Conspiracy theories often thrive in the absence of clear and conclusive evidence, filling the gaps with speculation and alternative narratives. In the case of Pearl Harbor, the emotional impact of the event, combined with the high stakes of World War II, has led to enduring interest and controversy.

In the decades since the attack, numerous investigations and studies have sought to uncover the truth about the forewarning claims. The most significant of these was the Congressional Joint Committee on the Investigation of the Pearl Harbor Attack, which conducted hearings in 1945-1946. The committee's findings were inconclusive, acknowledging failures in intelligence and preparedness but stopping short of concluding that there was a deliberate effort to allow the attack to happen.

More recent historical scholarship has continued to explore the complexities of the Pearl Harbor attack and the intelligence environment of the time. Historians such as Roberta Wohlstetter, in her seminal work "Pearl Harbor: Warning and Decision," have highlighted the challenges of intelligence analysis and the difficulties of distinguishing actionable intelligence from background noise. Wohlstetter's concept of "signal versus noise" remains a key framework for understanding the intelligence failures leading up to the attack.

Chapter 33: The Death of James Dean

James Dean, an iconic figure in American cinema, left an indelible mark on Hollywood and pop culture despite his tragically short career. His untimely death on September 30, 1955, at the age of 24, has been shrouded in mystery and speculation, leading to a plethora of theories and rumors about the true nature of the events that led to the fatal car crash. Dean's life and death have been the subject of intense scrutiny, fascination, and legend, making him a symbol of youthful rebellion and the fleeting nature of fame.

James Byron Dean was born on February 8, 1931, in Marion, Indiana. He grew up in a modest household and faced several hardships, including the death of his mother when he was nine years old. Raised by his aunt and uncle in Fairmount, Indiana, Dean developed an early interest in acting. He moved to Los Angeles to live with his father but eventually relocated to New York City to pursue his acting career more seriously. His breakthrough came with roles in television and on Broadway, which led to his discovery by Hollywood.

Dean's film career, though brief, was meteoric. He starred in only three major films: "East of Eden" (1955), "Rebel Without a Cause" (1955), and "Giant" (1956). These performances showcased his extraordinary talent and charismatic screen presence, earning him critical acclaim and a devoted fan base. His portrayal of troubled, rebellious youth resonated with audiences, cementing his status as a cultural icon.

Dean was also known for his passion for fast cars and racing. He owned several high-performance vehicles, including a Porsche 356 Speedster, which he raced in various competitions. In September 1955, Dean purchased a new Porsche 550 Spyder, which he affectionately nicknamed "Little Bastard." The car would soon become infamous as the vehicle in which he met his untimely end.

On September 30, 1955, Dean was driving his Porsche 550 Spyder to a race in Salinas, California, accompanied by his mechanic, Rolf Wütherich. They set off from Los Angeles in the early afternoon, planning to make the 300-mile journey in time for the weekend races. Dean and Wütherich were traveling north on U.S. Route 101 when they were stopped by a California Highway Patrol officer near Bakersfield for speeding. After receiving a warning, they continued their journey.

Around 5:45 PM, as they approached the junction of Route 466 (now State Route 46) and Route 41 near Cholame, California, a Ford Tudor driven by 23-year-old Donald Turnupseed was traveling in the opposite direction. Turnupseed made a left turn onto Route 41, directly into the path of Dean's oncoming Porsche. The two cars collided almost head-on, with the impact sending Dean's lightweight car spinning off the road. Dean suffered multiple severe injuries, including a broken neck, and was pronounced dead on arrival at Paso Robles War Memorial Hospital. Wütherich was thrown from the vehicle and survived with significant injuries, while Turnupseed sustained relatively minor injuries.

The official cause of the accident was attributed to Turnupseed's failure to see the fast-approaching Porsche, and no charges were filed against him. However, the circumstances surrounding the crash and Dean's death quickly became the subject of widespread speculation and conspiracy theories.

One of the most persistent theories suggests that Dean's Porsche was cursed. This notion gained traction due to the series of unfortunate events that befell those associated with the car both before and after the crash. The idea of the "curse" began with Dean's own premonitions about his death. Friends and colleagues reported that Dean had expressed a sense of foreboding in the days leading up to the accident, with some even recalling his eerie statements about not wanting to live past 25.

The supposed curse continued after Dean's death. The wreckage of the Porsche was purchased by Dr. William Eschrich, who salvaged parts of the car. Eschrich used the engine in his own race car, which was later involved in a serious accident. Another racer, Troy McHenry, used parts from Dean's car and was killed in a crash during a race. Additionally, the remains of the Porsche were displayed in various exhibitions, and several mysterious incidents, including fires and injuries, were reported by those who came into contact with the car. These events fueled the legend of the cursed "Little Bastard."

Another theory speculates that Dean's crash was the result of foul play. Some conspiracy theorists suggest that Dean was targeted because of his rising fame and the potential threat he posed to established stars in Hollywood. Others propose that the crash was orchestrated by individuals with grudges against Dean or those who stood to gain from his death. However, there is little concrete evidence to support these claims, and they remain in the realm of speculation.

Theories about mechanical failure also abound. Some experts have posited that the Porsche 550 Spyder, known for its high performance but also for being difficult to handle, may have experienced a mechanical failure that contributed to the crash. There have been suggestions that the car's steering or brakes might have malfunctioned, leading Dean to lose control at a critical moment. However, the exact cause of the crash remains unclear, as the car was too badly damaged to conduct a thorough investigation of its mechanical condition.

Dean's death also sparked a debate about the role of speed and driver behavior. Some critics argue that Dean's penchant for driving fast and his competitive nature may have played a significant role in the crash. Witnesses reported seeing the Porsche traveling at high speeds shortly before the collision, and Dean had a history of speeding tickets and reckless driving. This line of thinking suggests that Dean's own driving habits, combined with the challenging nature of the Porsche 550 Spyder, may have created a dangerous situation.

In the aftermath of Dean's death, his legacy only grew. He was posthumously awarded the first-ever Golden Globe for Best Motion Picture Actor in 1956, and he received two Academy Award nominations for Best Actor for his roles in "East of Eden" and "Giant." Dean became an enduring symbol of youthful rebellion, angst, and the transient nature of life and fame. His image and persona were immortalized in countless works of art, literature, and film, and he remains a cultural icon to this day.

The fascination with Dean's death also reflects broader themes in American culture, such as the allure of celebrity, the dangers of fast living, and the tragic hero narrative. Dean's story has been compared to other cultural icons who died young, such as Marilyn Monroe, Elvis Presley, and Kurt Cobain. Each of these figures left behind a legacy that was inextricably linked to their untimely deaths, and each has inspired similar speculation and myth-making.

James Dean's life and death continue to inspire countless books, documentaries, and articles, each attempting to unravel the mysteries and explore the impact of his brief but influential career. His death remains a poignant reminder of the fragility of life and the unpredictable nature of fame. Whether viewed through the lens of conspiracy, mechanical failure, or the inevitable risks of a high-speed lifestyle, the story of James Dean serves as a powerful cultural touchstone, capturing the imagination of generations and ensuring that his legend endures.

Chapter 34: The Sinking of the Titanic

The sinking of the RMS Titanic remains one of the most infamous maritime disasters in history, shrouded in mystery, intrigue, and numerous conspiracy theories. The Titanic, deemed "unsinkable" by its creators, was the largest and most luxurious ocean liner of its time. Constructed by the White Star Line, it set sail on its maiden voyage from Southampton to New York City on April 10, 1912, carrying some of the wealthiest individuals of the era, as well as hundreds of emigrants seeking a new life in America.

On the night of April 14, 1912, just four days into the voyage, the Titanic struck an iceberg in the North Atlantic Ocean. Despite the ship's advanced design and reputed unsinkability, the iceberg caused a fatal gash along its starboard side, leading to the flooding of its watertight compartments. As the ship began to take on water, it quickly became apparent that there were not enough lifeboats for all passengers and crew. The ensuing chaos and the frigid temperatures of the Atlantic exacerbated the tragedy, resulting in the deaths of more than 1,500 people.

The official inquiries conducted by both British and American authorities concluded that a combination of factors led to the disaster, including the high speed at which the Titanic was traveling through iceberg-laden waters, the inadequate number of lifeboats, and the lack of proper emergency procedures. However, these findings have not quelled the numerous conspiracy theories that have emerged over the decades.

One of the most persistent conspiracy theories suggests that the Titanic's sister ship, the RMS Olympic, was substituted for the Titanic in an elaborate insurance fraud scheme. Proponents of this theory argue that the Olympic, which had been damaged in a previous collision, was secretly disguised as the Titanic, and that the sinking was planned to claim insurance money. According to this theory, the real Titanic continued to operate under the guise of the Olympic. However, this theory lacks substantial evidence and is widely dismissed by experts.

Another intriguing theory involves the Federal Reserve. Some conspiracy theorists believe that powerful bankers opposed to the creation of the Federal Reserve were deliberately targeted in the disaster. Notable figures such as John Jacob Astor IV, Benjamin Guggenheim, and Isidor Straus, all of whom perished on the Titanic, were reportedly against the establishment of the Federal Reserve. The theory posits that their deaths were orchestrated to eliminate opposition and pave the way for the Federal Reserve's creation in December 1913. While this theory taps into broader suspicions about banking elites and their influence, it remains speculative and lacks concrete proof.

A more fantastical theory involves the idea that the Titanic was sunk by a German U-boat. Some suggest that the Titanic was mistakenly or intentionally targeted by a submarine, a notion fueled by the geopolitical tensions of the early 20th century. However, there is no historical evidence to support the presence of German submarines in the North Atlantic at the time of the sinking.

Additionally, there are theories that involve supernatural elements. Some believe the Titanic was cursed, pointing to the fact that it carried an Egyptian mummy, which was said to bring misfortune. This mummy, rumored to have been on board, supposedly unleashed its curse upon the ship, leading to its tragic fate. This theory, while captivating, is purely anecdotal and lacks any historical documentation.

The ship's design and construction have also been scrutinized. Some argue that the Titanic's builders used substandard materials, including brittle steel and weak rivets, which made the ship vulnerable to catastrophic damage upon striking the iceberg. While modern metallurgical analysis has provided some support for these claims, it is generally agreed that the primary cause of the sinking was the sheer size and impact of the iceberg itself.

The role of Captain Edward Smith has also been a focal point of controversy. Critics have questioned his decision to maintain high speeds despite ice warnings and his failure to take adequate evasive action. Some suggest that Smith was pressured by the White Star Line to make a record-breaking crossing, prioritizing speed over safety. This theory aligns with testimonies from surviving crew members who reported that Smith was aware of the icebergs but chose not to slow down. However, others defend Smith, arguing that he acted based on the best available information and that the true scale of the iceberg danger was underestimated.

The mysterious circumstances surrounding the Californian, a nearby ship, have further fueled conspiracy theories. The Californian reportedly stopped for the night due to ice concerns and was within visual range of the Titanic. Yet, its crew failed to respond to the Titanic's distress signals in time. This has led to speculation about the reasons behind their inaction. Some theorists suggest that the Californian's crew was part of a larger conspiracy, possibly involving a covert mission or orders to ignore the Titanic's plight. However, official investigations attributed the lack of response to miscommunication and human error rather than any malicious intent.

Despite these numerous theories, the most accepted explanation remains that the Titanic's sinking was a tragic accident resulting from a convergence of unfortunate circumstances. Advances in maritime safety regulations, such as the International Convention for the Safety of Life at Sea (SOLAS), were established in response to the disaster, mandating sufficient lifeboats and improved ship designs.

In recent years, technological advancements have allowed for extensive exploration of the Titanic's wreck, lying over two miles beneath the ocean's surface. These expeditions have provided invaluable insights into the ship's final moments and the conditions of its sinking.

However, they have also stirred new debates about the preservation of the site and the ethical considerations of salvaging artifacts from the wreck.

The Titanic disaster continues to captivate the public imagination, symbolizing human hubris and the perils of technological overconfidence. Its story has been immortalized in countless books, documentaries, and films, most notably James Cameron's 1997 blockbuster "Titanic," which brought the tragedy to a new generation. The enduring fascination with the Titanic ensures that its legacy will persist, blending historical fact with the allure of mystery and conspiracy.

Chapter 35: The Secret of Oak Island

The Secret of Oak Island has captured the imaginations of treasure hunters and historians for over two centuries. Located off the coast of Nova Scotia, Canada, Oak Island is the site of one of the world's longest-running treasure hunts, fueled by rumors of buried riches and mysterious artifacts. The island's lore begins in 1795 when three young men discovered a depression in the ground under a large oak tree, which had a tackle block hanging from one of its branches. Suspecting that they had stumbled upon a hidden treasure, they began digging, only to find layers of logs every ten feet, suggesting a man-made structure beneath the surface.

As the young men dug deeper, they encountered more wooden platforms, along with layers of charcoal, putty, and coconut fibers, none of which were native to the island. These discoveries indicated that a significant effort had been made to conceal whatever lay below. The men reached a depth of about 30 feet before their progress was halted by water flooding into the pit. This flooding has been a recurring challenge for treasure hunters on Oak Island, leading to the theory that the pit is booby-trapped with underground flood tunnels designed to thwart excavations.

The mystery of Oak Island, often referred to as the "Money Pit," has attracted numerous expeditions over the years, each attempting to solve the enigma and claim the treasure that is believed to be buried there. One of the earliest documented efforts was led by the Onslow Company in 1804, which dug to a depth of 90 feet before being forced to abandon their efforts due to flooding. Their findings included a stone inscribed with strange symbols, which has since become a focal point of the island's mystery. While the stone's original inscription has been lost, various translations suggest it warned of the pit's traps or hinted at the presence of treasure below.

Throughout the 19th and 20th centuries, numerous other attempts were made to uncover the island's secrets. The Truro Company, for instance, encountered layers of oak platforms and clay, as well as coconut fibers, which some theorists believe were used to construct the flood tunnels. The company reached a depth of 98 feet before being defeated by water. In the early 1900s, another significant expedition led by Frederick Blair and the Oak Island Association involved the use of modern drilling equipment. They managed to bring up samples of what appeared to be oak wood and coconut fiber from depths of over 100 feet, further fueling speculation that something valuable lay beneath.

Several theories have been proposed regarding the origin and nature of the Oak Island treasure. One of the most popular suggests that it is the hidden stash of the infamous pirate Captain Kidd, who was known to bury his loot in secret locations. Another theory posits that the treasure is linked to the Knights Templar, a medieval Christian military order rumored to have amassed great wealth and knowledge. Some proponents of this theory believe that the Templars hid their treasure, possibly including religious artifacts such as the Holy Grail or the Ark of the Covenant, on Oak Island.

Other theories suggest that the island's secrets could be linked to Freemasonry, given the various Masonic symbols reportedly found on the island. Some even speculate that the pit might contain lost works of literature, such as the missing manuscripts of William Shakespeare, believed by some to have been authored by Francis Bacon, who was known to use ciphers and codes in his works. The idea that Bacon, a prominent figure in the early 17th century, could have hidden his works on Oak Island aligns with the notion that the Money Pit is a highly sophisticated trap designed to protect valuable items.

Modern excavations have continued to yield tantalizing clues, although no definitive treasure has been uncovered. In the 1960s, a group led by Robert Dunfield used heavy machinery to excavate the site, uncovering various artifacts, including a pair of scissors, an iron ruler, and a fragment of chain. More recently, the efforts of brothers Rick and Marty Lagina, documented in the History Channel's series "The Curse of Oak Island," have brought renewed attention to the mystery. Their team has utilized advanced technology, including ground-penetrating radar and sonar, to explore the depths of the Money Pit and surrounding areas.

The Laginas' efforts have revealed a complex network of tunnels and cavities, suggesting that the original builders went to great lengths to construct an elaborate underground system. Among their discoveries are ancient coins, metal fragments, and wooden structures that have been carbon-dated to the 17th century, aligning with some of the historical theories about the treasure's origin. The team has also found evidence of human activity, such as iron spikes and pickaxe marks, indicating that the pit and its tunnels were indeed man-made.

In addition to the physical challenges of excavation, the Oak Island mystery is compounded by legal and financial hurdles. Over the years, treasure hunters have faced disputes over land ownership and the distribution of any potential findings. The Nova Scotia government has implemented regulations to preserve the historical and archaeological significance of the site, requiring permits and oversight for any excavation activities. These legal complexities add another layer of difficulty to an already daunting quest.

The allure of Oak Island lies not only in the potential for material wealth but also in the intellectual challenge of unraveling its secrets. Theories about the island's true purpose and the identities of its original builders continue to evolve as new evidence emerges. Some researchers suggest that the island may have served as a hiding place for important documents or artifacts during tumultuous periods of history, such as the English Civil War or the American Revolution.

Despite the numerous failed attempts and setbacks, the quest for the Oak Island treasure persists. Each new discovery, no matter how small, adds to the island's rich tapestry of history and intrigue. The combination of historical clues, enigmatic artifacts, and the enduring mystery of the Money Pit ensures that Oak Island will remain a subject of fascination and speculation for generations to come. The story of Oak Island is a testament to human curiosity and the enduring allure of hidden treasure, reflecting our timeless desire to uncover the unknown and solve the riddles of the past.

Chapter 36: The Dyatlov Pass Incident

The Dyatlov Pass Incident is one of the most perplexing and enduring mysteries of the 20th century. In late January 1959, a group of nine experienced Soviet hikers led by Igor Dyatlov embarked on a challenging expedition through the Ural Mountains. The goal was to reach Otorten, a mountain whose name in the indigenous Mansi language ominously means "Don't go there." The group consisted of eight men and two women, all of whom were seasoned hikers and students or graduates of the Ural Polytechnic Institute.

The hikers set out from the small settlement of Vizhai on January 27, 1959. Their journey progressed smoothly until they encountered a snowstorm on February 1, which forced them to deviate from their planned route and make camp on the eastern slopes of Kholat Syakhl, a mountain whose name translates to "Dead Mountain." This deviation set the stage for the tragedy that would unfold.

When the group failed to return as scheduled on February 12, search and rescue teams were dispatched. It wasn't until February 26 that searchers discovered the group's abandoned and badly damaged tent on Kholat Syakhl. The tent was found cut open from the inside, and the hikers' belongings, including shoes and warm clothing, were left behind, indicating a sudden and desperate escape. Footprints leading away from the tent were found, suggesting that some members fled in socks, barefoot, or wearing only a single shoe.

As rescuers followed the trail of footprints, they soon discovered the bodies of Yuri Krivonischenko and Yuri Doroshenko, the first two victims, near a tree at the edge of a forest approximately a mile from the tent. Both were shoeless and dressed only in their underwear. It appeared they had attempted to build a fire before succumbing to the extreme cold. The branches on the tree were broken up to five meters high, suggesting that someone had climbed it, possibly to look for something or to escape from a threat.

Three more bodies, those of Dyatlov, Rustem Slobodin, and Zinaida Kolmogorova, were found at varying distances between the tent and the tree. Dyatlov was found with his arms around a tree branch, as if attempting to climb. Slobodin's body bore a small crack in his skull, though it was not deemed a fatal injury. Kolmogorova's body displayed signs of struggle, with bruises and abrasions. Their positions suggested they had been attempting to return to the tent when they died of hypothermia.

The remaining four hikers, Aleksander Kolevatov, Lyudmila Dubinina, Nikolai Thibeaux-Brignolles, and Semyon Zolotaryov, were not found until May 4, under four meters of snow in a ravine further into the forest. These bodies presented even more baffling evidence. Dubinina and Zolotaryov had major chest fractures, while Thibeaux-Brignolles had a severe skull fracture. The force required to cause such injuries was compared to that of a car crash, and it was noted that there were no external wounds associated with these fractures. Additionally, Dubinina was found missing her tongue, eyes, and part of her lips, raising further questions about the nature of their deaths.

The official Soviet investigation concluded that an "unknown compelling force" had caused the deaths of the hikers. The lack of concrete answers gave rise to numerous theories and speculations over the decades. Some suggested an avalanche might have forced the hikers to flee their tent, but this theory has been contested due to the shallow slope of the mountain and the lack of typical avalanche debris. Moreover, the injuries sustained by the victims were not consistent with avalanche trauma.

Other theories proposed include infrasound-induced panic, where the wind passing over the mountain could have generated infrasound waves that induced feelings of unease and terror in the hikers, prompting them to flee their tent in a state of panic. While plausible, this theory does not account for the severe physical injuries observed.

Another popular theory involves military testing. Some speculate that the hikers stumbled upon a secret Soviet military experiment, possibly involving parachute mines or radiological weapons. Support for this theory includes reports of strange orange spheres in the sky observed by another group of hikers in the area on the same night and traces of radiation found on some of the victims' clothing. However, there is no definitive evidence linking these factors to the incident.

The indigenous Mansi people, who inhabit the region, have also been subjects of suspicion. Some early investigators theorized that the hikers might have been attacked by Mansi hunters for trespassing on sacred land. However, this theory was quickly dismissed due to the lack of defensive wounds and the peaceful nature of the Mansi.

In recent years, new investigations and advancements in technology have offered fresh insights, though no conclusive answers. In 2019, the Russian government reopened the case, focusing on natural causes like avalanches and snow slabs. This renewed investigation concluded in 2020, reaffirming the theory that an avalanche or similar natural event likely caused the hikers to panic and flee their tent. However, critics argue that this explanation still does not fully account for the specific injuries and the absence of typical avalanche indicators.

The Dyatlov Pass Incident remains a topic of fascination and debate, with each theory raising as many questions as it answers. The enigmatic combination of sudden, unexplained flight from the tent, severe and unusual injuries, and the apparent lack of a definitive cause of death continues to baffle experts and amateurs alike. As with many enduring mysteries, the allure lies in the gaps between the known facts, where speculation and imagination can roam freely. The story of the Dyatlov Pass Incident endures as a testament to the human drive to seek answers, even in the face of insurmountable uncertainty.

Chapter 37: The Lost Colony of Roanoke

The Lost Colony of Roanoke is one of the oldest and most enduring mysteries in American history. In 1587, a group of English settlers established a colony on Roanoke Island, off the coast of what is now North Carolina. This colony, sponsored by Sir Walter Raleigh, was intended to be the first permanent English settlement in the New World. However, when a supply ship returned to the colony in 1590, the settlers had vanished without a trace, leaving behind only a cryptic clue: the word "CROATOAN" carved into a post.

The story of Roanoke begins with England's ambitions to expand its influence and compete with Spain's dominant presence in the Americas. In 1584, Queen Elizabeth I granted a charter to Sir Walter Raleigh to explore and colonize the land in North America. Raleigh sent reconnaissance expeditions in 1584 and 1585 to survey the area and establish relations with local Native American tribes. These initial expeditions chose Roanoke Island as the site for the new colony, owing to its strategic location and favorable environment.

In 1587, Raleigh dispatched a group of approximately 115 settlers, including men, women, and children, under the leadership of John White, a skilled artist and cartographer. Among the settlers were White's daughter, Eleanor Dare, and her husband, Ananias Dare. Eleanor gave birth to Virginia Dare, the first English child born in the New World, on August 18, 1587. This birth symbolized the hopes and aspirations of the English colonists to establish a lasting presence in America.

Upon their arrival, the settlers discovered that the previous colony, established in 1585, had been abandoned, with only skeletal remains left behind. This earlier group had suffered from a lack of supplies and strained relations with the local Algonquian tribes. Despite these ominous signs, the new settlers rebuilt the colony and attempted to establish friendly relations with the indigenous peoples, including the Croatan tribe, who lived on nearby Hatteras Island.

Shortly after the new colony was established, John White returned to England to procure additional supplies and reinforcements. His departure was ill-timed, as England was on the brink of war with Spain. The impending threat of the Spanish Armada in 1588 delayed White's return to Roanoke. It was not until August 1590, three years after his departure, that White finally secured passage back to the colony with a supply ship.

When White and his crew arrived at Roanoke Island, they found the settlement deserted. There were no signs of struggle or violence, but all the houses and fortifications had been dismantled. The only clue was the word "CROATOAN" carved into a post and the letters "CRO" carved into a nearby tree. White interpreted this as a message indicating that the colonists had relocated to Croatoan Island, known today as Hatteras Island. However, inclement weather and logistical challenges prevented White from immediately searching for the settlers, and he was forced to return to England without further investigation.

The fate of the Roanoke colonists has since been the subject of extensive speculation and research, spawning numerous theories and hypotheses. One prevalent theory is that the settlers integrated with local Native American tribes to survive. The Croatan tribe, in particular, is often mentioned in this context. Some historians believe that the colonists sought refuge with the Croatans and were absorbed into their community, adopting their customs and intermarrying with them. This theory is supported by later accounts of European settlers encountering Native American tribes with English-sounding names and European features, as well as reports of indigenous people speaking broken English.

Another theory suggests that the colonists attempted to move inland, possibly to the Chesapeake Bay area, where Raleigh had intended to establish a more permanent settlement. Archaeological evidence and historical records indicate that the English had some knowledge of the Chesapeake region and its potential for supporting a larger colony. However, there is little concrete evidence to confirm that the Roanoke settlers made such a journey or established a new settlement there.

Some researchers propose that the settlers met with a violent end, either at the hands of hostile Native American tribes or due to internal strife and resource shortages. The region was known for its complex and often volatile relationships between different indigenous groups, and the arrival of European settlers added another layer of tension. The colonists' lack of supplies and support from England would have made them vulnerable to both external and internal conflicts.

In recent years, advances in archaeology and technology have offered new insights into the mystery of Roanoke. Excavations on both Roanoke Island and Hatteras Island have uncovered artifacts that suggest a prolonged presence of European settlers, including pieces of English pottery, metal tools, and other items dating to the late 16th century. These findings lend some credence to the theory that the colonists may have dispersed and lived among Native American tribes for an extended period.

Genetic research has also been proposed as a means of unraveling the mystery. By analyzing the DNA of contemporary descendants of Native American tribes in the region, researchers hope to identify any genetic markers that may indicate intermingling with the Roanoke colonists. While this approach holds promise, it also presents significant challenges due to the complex history of population movements and interactions in the area over the centuries.

The Lost Colony of Roanoke continues to captivate the public imagination and inspire scholarly inquiry. Its story is a poignant reminder of the challenges and uncertainties faced by early European explorers and settlers in the New World. The combination of hope, ambition, and mystery surrounding Roanoke has cemented its place in American folklore and historical research.

The legacy of the Lost Colony extends beyond its immediate historical context. It has influenced literature, art, and popular culture, serving as a symbol of the enduring quest for discovery and understanding. From novels and plays to documentaries and television series, the mystery of Roanoke has been explored and reimagined in countless ways, each interpretation adding to the rich tapestry of the legend.

The fate of the Roanoke colonists remains one of the most tantalizing puzzles in American history. Despite centuries of investigation and speculation, definitive answers continue to elude researchers. The word "CROATOAN" carved into a post stands as a silent testament to the colonists' last known act, a cryptic message that has intrigued and baffled generations. As new methods and technologies emerge, there is hope that one day the mystery of the Lost Colony will be resolved, providing closure to one of history's most enigmatic chapters. Until then, the story of Roanoke endures as a symbol of the human spirit's resilience and the perpetual quest for knowledge and understanding.

Chapter 38: The Real Story of Jack the Ripper

The real story of Jack the Ripper is a dark and enigmatic chapter in the annals of criminal history, filled with grisly murders, mysterious letters, and countless theories that have captured the public imagination for over a century. The name "Jack the Ripper" evokes images of a shadowy figure stalking the fog-laden streets of Victorian London, targeting vulnerable women in the impoverished district of Whitechapel. The Ripper's identity has remained one of the most notorious unsolved mysteries in the history of crime, with numerous suspects, theories, and controversies surrounding the case.

The gruesome saga began in 1888, a year marked by social unrest, economic hardship, and rising crime rates in London. Whitechapel, located in the East End, was a neighborhood plagued by poverty, overcrowding, and unsanitary living conditions. Many of its residents, particularly women, turned to prostitution to survive. It was against this backdrop that a series of brutal murders occurred, each more horrifying than the last.

The first canonical victim, Mary Ann Nichols, was found in the early hours of August 31, 1888. Her body was discovered in Buck's Row (now Durward Street), with her throat slashed and her abdomen mutilated. Just over a week later, on September 8, the body of Annie Chapman was found in the backyard of 29 Hanbury Street. Like Nichols, Chapman had her throat cut and her abdomen savagely mutilated, with parts of her organs removed.

The Ripper's killing spree escalated on the night of September 30, known as the "Double Event." Elizabeth Stride was found dead in Dutfield's Yard off Berner Street (now Henriques Street), with a single deep cut to her throat. Unlike the previous victims, Stride's body showed no signs of mutilation, leading some to speculate that the

Ripper was interrupted. Less than an hour later, the body of Catherine Eddowes was discovered in Mitre Square. Eddowes had suffered the same fate as Nichols and Chapman, with extensive mutilations to her face and abdomen, and her kidney and uterus removed.

The final canonical victim, Mary Jane Kelly, was found on November 9 in her room at Miller's Court, Dorset Street. Kelly's murder was the most brutal of all; her body was extensively mutilated, with her face almost unrecognizable and her organs scattered around the room. The sheer savagery of the attack indicated that the Ripper had spent a significant amount of time with the victim, further baffling the authorities.

The investigation into the murders was plagued by a lack of forensic tools and the primitive state of police procedures at the time. The Metropolitan Police, led by Commissioner Sir Charles Warren, and the City of London Police, were both involved in the hunt for the killer. However, jurisdictional issues, poor communication, and public pressure hampered their efforts. The police received hundreds of letters from individuals claiming to be the Ripper, but only a few are considered significant.

Among these letters, the "Dear Boss" letter, received by the Central News Agency on September 27, 1888, stands out. Signed "Jack the Ripper," it taunted the police and threatened more murders. Another notable letter, the "Saucy Jacky" postcard, was received on October 1, describing the "Double Event" and boasting about the murders. Perhaps the most chilling communication was the "From Hell" letter, received by George Lusk of the Whitechapel Vigilance Committee on October 16, accompanied by a small box containing a piece of a human kidney. The letter's author claimed to have fried and eaten the other half of the kidney, allegedly taken from Catherine Eddowes.

Despite the extensive manhunt, numerous suspects, and mounting public hysteria, the identity of Jack the Ripper remained elusive. Over the years, countless theories and suspects have been proposed, ranging from plausible to fantastical. One of the most widely discussed suspects was Montague John Druitt, a barrister and teacher whose suicide in December 1888 coincided with the end of the murders. Druitt's family reportedly believed he was the Ripper, and he had a history of mental illness. However, there is little concrete evidence linking him to the crimes.

Another prominent suspect was Aaron Kosminski, a Polish Jew and resident of Whitechapel who was committed to an asylum in 1891. Kosminski was named as a suspect by several high-ranking police officials, including Chief Inspector Donald Swanson and Assistant Commissioner Sir Robert Anderson. In recent years, DNA analysis of a shawl purportedly found at the scene of Catherine Eddowes' murder linked Kosminski to the crime. However, the reliability of the shawl's provenance and the DNA evidence has been widely debated.

Dr. Francis Tumblety, an American quack doctor who was in London at the time of the murders, was also considered a suspect. Tumblety had a history of misogyny and was arrested in November 1888 for unrelated offenses. He fled to the United States shortly after his release on bail, raising suspicions about his involvement. However, there is no definitive evidence to connect him to the Ripper murders.

Other suspects include Sir William Gull, Queen Victoria's physician, who is central to various conspiracy theories involving Freemasons and a supposed royal cover-up. The theory suggests that the murders were part of a plot to silence those who knew about the secret marriage of Prince Albert Victor to a Catholic woman. This theory, popularized by the book "Jack the Ripper: The Final Solution" by Stephen Knight, has been largely discredited by historians.

More recent theories have suggested figures such as Walter Sickert, a British artist whose paintings allegedly contain clues about the murders, and James Maybrick, a Liverpool cotton merchant whose alleged diary confessed to being the Ripper. Both theories have sparked significant debate and skepticism among experts.

The social and cultural context of the Ripper murders is crucial to understanding their impact. Victorian London was a city of stark contrasts, with immense wealth and profound poverty existing side by side. The East End, where the murders occurred, was notorious for its destitution, overcrowding, and vice. The Ripper's victims were all women of low social standing, often involved in prostitution, highlighting the vulnerability and marginalization of these women in Victorian society.

The press played a significant role in shaping public perception of the murders. Sensationalist reporting, graphic illustrations, and lurid details fueled widespread panic and fascination. The Ripper became a symbol of the dangers lurking in the dark alleys of London, and the case highlighted the inadequacies of the police force and the need for social reform.

The legacy of Jack the Ripper extends beyond the gruesome events of 1888. The case has inspired countless books, films, documentaries, and works of fiction, making it one of the most analyzed and debated topics in criminology. The image of the Ripper, clad in a dark coat and top hat, has become an enduring figure in popular culture, representing both the fear of the unknown and the fascination with unsolved mysteries.

Modern investigative techniques, such as criminal profiling and forensic science, have been applied to the case in attempts to uncover new evidence and offer fresh perspectives. However, the lack of contemporary forensic evidence and the passage of time have made it challenging to reach definitive conclusions.

Despite the numerous theories and suspects, the true identity of Jack the Ripper remains unknown. The case endures as a haunting reminder of the dark side of human nature and the enduring quest for justice. The fascination with the Ripper is not merely about the gruesome nature of the crimes but also about the enduring mystery and the many unanswered questions that continue to captivate the imagination.

The real story of Jack the Ripper is a complex tapestry of historical fact, speculation, and myth. It is a story that has transcended its immediate context to become a symbol of the ultimate unsolved mystery. As long as the identity of the Ripper remains unknown, the case will continue to intrigue, perplex, and inspire those who seek to uncover the truth behind one of history's most infamous murderers.

Chapter 39: The Disappearance of Jimmy Hoffa

The disappearance of Jimmy Hoffa remains one of the most enduring and captivating mysteries in American history. Hoffa, a charismatic and controversial labor leader, was last seen on July 30, 1975, outside the Machus Red Fox restaurant in Bloomfield Township, Michigan. His sudden and unexplained disappearance sparked a massive investigation, countless theories, and a fascination that endures to this day. To fully understand the significance of Hoffa's disappearance, one must delve into his life, the era in which he lived, and the powerful forces that surrounded him.

James Riddle Hoffa, born on February 14, 1913, in Brazil, Indiana, rose to prominence as a labor organizer and eventually became the president of the International Brotherhood of Teamsters (IBT), one of the most powerful unions in the United States. Hoffa's early life was marked by poverty and hardship. His father, a coal miner, died when Hoffa was just seven years old, leaving his mother to raise him and his siblings. Hoffa dropped out of school at 14 to work and help support his family, a decision that would shape his future as a labor leader.

Hoffa's journey into labor organizing began in the 1930s, during the Great Depression. He started working as a warehouseman in Detroit, Michigan, where he became involved in labor disputes and strikes. His natural leadership abilities and fierce determination quickly made him a prominent figure in the local labor movement. Hoffa's rise within the Teamsters was rapid; he became a full-time organizer in the early 1940s and soon took on more significant roles within the union.

By 1952, Hoffa had ascended to the position of national vice-president of the Teamsters. His leadership style was marked by a combination of charisma, shrewd negotiating skills, and a willingness to confront management head-on. Hoffa's tenure as Teamsters president, beginning in 1957, saw the union grow in size and influence, becoming a dominant force in American labor. Under his leadership, the Teamsters secured better wages, working conditions, and benefits for its members.

However, Hoffa's methods and associations also drew significant controversy and scrutiny. He was known for his connections to organized crime figures, who saw the powerful union as a lucrative avenue for control and profit. Hoffa's willingness to work with mobsters to achieve his goals made him a target for law enforcement and political figures alike. His relationships with figures like Anthony "Tony Pro" Provenzano, a notorious New Jersey mobster and former Teamsters vice-president, would later play a critical role in his disappearance.

Hoffa's legal troubles began in earnest in the late 1950s and 1960s. He was indicted several times on charges ranging from jury tampering to bribery and fraud. In 1967, he was convicted of attempted bribery of a grand juror and sentenced to 15 years in prison. Despite his imprisonment, Hoffa remained a powerful and influential figure within the Teamsters. He continued to control the union from behind bars, and his ambitions for a return to power never waned.

In 1971, Hoffa struck a deal with President Richard Nixon, securing a commutation of his sentence. The conditions of his release included an agreement to stay out of union activities until 1980. Hoffa, however, had no intention of honoring this agreement. He immediately began planning his return to the Teamsters' leadership, setting the stage for his eventual disappearance.

On the day he vanished, Hoffa was scheduled to meet with Anthony Provenzano and Anthony Giacalone, a Detroit mobster, at the Machus Red Fox restaurant. Hoffa was seen waiting in the parking lot of the restaurant around 2:30 p.m. by several witnesses. By 2:45 p.m., he was gone. His car, a dark green Pontiac Grand Ville, was found in the restaurant parking lot, but there was no sign of Hoffa. Despite extensive searches and investigations, his body was never found, and no one was ever charged in connection with his disappearance.

The mystery of what happened to Jimmy Hoffa has given rise to numerous theories, each as compelling as it is speculative. One of the most prevalent theories is that Hoffa was murdered by mobsters who feared his return to power would disrupt their control over the Teamsters. Hoffa's connections to organized crime, particularly his strained relationship with Provenzano, are often cited as motives for his disappearance. Provenzano had a well-documented history of violence and a falling out with Hoffa, leading many to believe that he played a central role in the plot to kill him.

Another theory suggests that Hoffa was killed and his body disposed of in a manner designed to ensure it would never be found. Various locations have been suggested as potential burial sites, including a landfill in New Jersey, a concrete slab under Giants Stadium in East Rutherford, New Jersey, and a horse farm in Michigan. Despite extensive searches and investigations, none of these locations have yielded definitive evidence of Hoffa's remains.

Over the years, numerous individuals have come forward claiming to have knowledge of Hoffa's fate. One of the most notable confessions came from Frank "The Irishman" Sheeran, a labor union official and mob hitman. In his book "I Heard You Paint Houses," Sheeran claimed to have killed Hoffa on orders from mob bosses and disposed of his body. However, Sheeran's account has been met with skepticism and has not been substantiated by physical evidence.

The FBI and other law enforcement agencies have conducted extensive investigations into Hoffa's disappearance, but the case remains officially unsolved. In 2006, the FBI conducted a high-profile search of a horse farm in Milford Township, Michigan, based on information provided by a mob informant. The search, which involved digging up the ground with heavy machinery, ultimately yielded no evidence.

The mystery of Jimmy Hoffa's disappearance continues to capture the public's imagination, partly because it encapsulates a fascinating era in American history. The 1970s were a time of significant social and political upheaval, marked by corruption, organized crime, and labor unrest. Hoffa's life and career were emblematic of these broader trends, and his disappearance serves as a poignant reminder of the darker aspects of American society during this period.

In recent years, advances in forensic technology and new investigative techniques have offered some hope that the mystery might one day be solved. DNA testing, ground-penetrating radar, and other modern tools have been employed in various searches, although none have yet provided conclusive results. The passage of time has also seen many of the key figures involved in the case pass away, taking their secrets with them.

The legacy of Jimmy Hoffa's disappearance extends beyond the specifics of the case itself. Hoffa's life and career have been the subject of numerous books, films, and documentaries, each offering different interpretations of his impact on American labor and his mysterious fate. Martin Scorsese's 2019 film "The Irishman," based on Sheeran's account, brought renewed attention to the case and introduced Hoffa's story to a new generation.

Ultimately, the disappearance of Jimmy Hoffa remains one of the most compelling and enduring mysteries in American history. It is a story of ambition, power, corruption, and the dark underbelly of the American Dream. As long as the case remains unsolved, it will continue to fascinate and intrigue, serving as a reminder of the enigmatic figure at its center and the turbulent era in which he lived.

Chapter 40: The Salem Witch Trials

The Salem Witch Trials, a dark and tumultuous chapter in American history, began in the spring of 1692 in the colonial Massachusetts town of Salem Village, now Danvers. This infamous episode of mass hysteria, religious fervor, and judicial overreach resulted in the execution of twenty people, mostly women, and the imprisonment of many others. To understand the complex social, political, and cultural context that fueled the Salem Witch Trials, one must delve into the Puritan belief system, the specific events leading up to the trials, the key players involved, and the lasting impact of this tragic period.

The Puritans, who founded the Massachusetts Bay Colony, were a religious group that sought to purify the Church of England and create a theocratic society based on their strict interpretation of the Bible. They believed in the existence of witches—individuals, often women, who had made a pact with the Devil and used supernatural powers to harm others. This belief in witchcraft was not unique to the Puritans; it was a widespread notion in Europe and had led to numerous witch hunts and executions throughout the 16th and 17th centuries. However, the intensity and scale of the Salem witch trials were unparalleled in colonial America.

Salem Village in the late 17th century was a community fraught with tension and division. Disputes over land ownership, church politics, and personal rivalries created an environment ripe for conflict. The village was also experiencing the aftershocks of King Philip's War, a brutal conflict between Native American tribes and English settlers, which had left many families grieving and anxious about the future. Economic hardships and the harsh realities of frontier life further contributed to the community's sense of instability and fear.

The spark that ignited the Salem witch trials came in January 1692, when nine-year-old Elizabeth "Betty" Parris and her eleven-year-old cousin Abigail Williams, the daughter and niece of Reverend Samuel

Parris, began exhibiting strange behaviors. They experienced fits, contortions, and outbursts that the local physician, Dr. William Griggs, attributed to bewitchment. As news of the girls' affliction spread, other young girls in the village, including Ann Putnam Jr., Mercy Lewis, Elizabeth Hubbard, Mary Walcott, and Mary Warren, began displaying similar symptoms.

Under pressure to identify the source of their torment, the girls named several women as their tormentors. The first three women accused were Tituba, an enslaved woman of Caribbean or African descent who worked in the Parris household; Sarah Good, a destitute beggar; and Sarah Osborne, an elderly woman who had not attended church regularly. These women were easy targets due to their marginalized status in the community.

The initial hearings and examinations took place in Salem Village in March 1692. The proceedings were led by local magistrates Jonathan Corwin and John Hathorne, who aggressively interrogated the accused. Tituba's confession under duress, in which she claimed to have been coerced by the Devil and implicated others in a witch conspiracy, fueled the hysteria. Her vivid descriptions of black dogs, yellow birds, and spectral evidence—a form of evidence based on visions and dreams—convinced many that a sinister plot was afoot.

As accusations multiplied, the scope of the witch hunt expanded beyond Salem Village to neighboring towns. The newly appointed governor of Massachusetts, Sir William Phips, established the Special Court of Oyer and Terminer to handle the burgeoning number of cases. This court, presided over by judges including Samuel Sewall, William Stoughton, and Samuel Phips, operated with a sense of urgency and a conviction that the Devil was at work in the colony.

The trials were marked by sensational testimonies and dubious evidence. The afflicted girls' dramatic fits and accusations, along with spectral evidence, were given significant weight. Spectral evidence was particularly controversial, as it involved claims that the spirits or specters of the accused were seen committing witchcraft, even if the accused were physically elsewhere at the time. This type of evidence was notoriously unreliable, but in the atmosphere of fear and superstition, it was often decisive.

One of the most infamous cases was that of Rebecca Nurse, a respected elderly woman known for her piety and virtue. Despite a petition signed by many villagers attesting to her innocence, Nurse was found guilty based largely on the spectral evidence and the testimonies of the afflicted girls. Her conviction and execution on July 19, 1692, shocked the community and raised doubts about the legitimacy of the trials.

The trials reached their peak in the summer of 1692, with a series of rapid convictions and executions. Bridget Bishop, the first person to be executed, was hanged on June 10, 1692. In total, nineteen people were hanged, and one man, Giles Corey, was pressed to death with heavy stones for refusing to enter a plea. Corey's refusal was a protest against the court's methods and an attempt to prevent his property from being seized by the state, which would have left his family destitute.

By the fall of 1692, public opinion began to turn against the trials. Prominent ministers, including Increase Mather and his son Cotton Mather, who initially supported the trials, started to voice concerns about the use of spectral evidence and the validity of the accusations. Increase Mather's publication "Cases of Conscience Concerning Evil Spirits" argued against the reliance on spectral evidence, emphasizing that it was better for ten suspected witches to escape than for one innocent person to be condemned.

Governor Phips, influenced by these arguments and the growing backlash, dissolved the Court of Oyer and Terminer in October 1692 and replaced it with a new court that disallowed spectral evidence. This new court, the Superior Court of Judicature, reviewed the remaining cases and acquitted many of the accused. The witch trials gradually came to an end, and the last executions took place in September 1692.

In the aftermath of the trials, the colony grappled with the consequences of the hysteria. Many of the convicted witches had their sentences posthumously reversed, and financial restitution was made to their families. Samuel Sewall, one of the judges, publicly confessed his guilt and shame for his role in the trials. In a powerful act of contrition, he stood before his congregation in Boston's Old South Meeting House in 1697 and read a statement acknowledging his error and seeking forgiveness.

The Salem Witch Trials have left a lasting legacy in American history and culture. They serve as a stark reminder of the dangers of mass hysteria, scapegoating, and the abuse of judicial power. The trials have been the subject of numerous works of literature, including Arthur Miller's play "The Crucible," which uses the events as an allegory for the McCarthy-era Red Scare and the persecution of alleged communists in the 1950s.

Historians have continued to study the Salem Witch Trials, offering various interpretations and explanations for the events. Some have pointed to the social, economic, and religious tensions within the community as contributing factors. The role of gender has also been examined, as the majority of the accused were women who defied the traditional roles and expectations of Puritan society. Psychological theories, such as mass hysteria and the influence of ergot poisoning (a hallucinogenic fungus found in rye), have also been proposed.

The physical sites associated with the trials, including the Salem Witch House (the former home of Judge Jonathan Corwin) and the Salem Witch Trials Memorial, attract visitors and serve as educational resources. These sites, along with museums and historical societies, work to preserve the memory of the victims and educate the public about the trials' historical context and significance.

The Salem Witch Trials stand as a cautionary tale about the perils of intolerance, fear, and the breakdown of due process. They remind us of the importance of critical thinking, skepticism, and the protection of individual rights in the face of collective paranoia. The legacy of the trials continues to resonate, serving as a powerful example of how societal pressures and unfounded accusations can lead to tragic consequences.

174

Chapter 41: The Death of Michael Jackson

The death of Michael Jackson on June 25, 2009, sent shockwaves around the world and marked the end of an era for one of the most influential and controversial figures in the history of popular music. Known as the "King of Pop," Michael Jackson's life was a blend of extraordinary talent, staggering success, personal turmoil, and relentless media scrutiny. His death at the age of 50 was not just the passing of a global icon but also the culmination of a series of complex events that revealed much about the pressures and pitfalls of fame.

Michael Joseph Jackson was born on August 29, 1958, in Gary, Indiana. He was the eighth of ten children in the Jackson family, a working-class African-American family. From a young age, Michael exhibited a remarkable talent for music and dance. He and his brothers formed the Jackson 5, a group that quickly rose to fame under the management of their father, Joe Jackson. The Jackson 5 became known for their catchy pop-soul hits and Michael's dynamic stage presence.

As Michael grew older, he embarked on a solo career that would establish him as one of the greatest entertainers of all time. His 1982 album "Thriller" remains the best-selling album in history, with iconic tracks like "Billie Jean," "Beat It," and the title song, "Thriller." Jackson's innovative music videos and his signature dance moves, particularly the moonwalk, cemented his status as a global superstar.

However, Jackson's personal life was marred by controversy and legal issues. He faced numerous allegations of child sexual abuse, which he consistently denied. In 1993, he was accused by a 13-year-old boy, Jordan Chandler, but the case was settled out of court. A more serious legal battle ensued in 2005 when he was tried and acquitted on charges of molesting another boy, Gavin Arvizo. These accusations and the intense media coverage took a significant toll on Jackson's reputation and mental health.

In the years leading up to his death, Jackson's financial troubles and health issues became more pronounced. Despite earning millions, he faced mounting debt due to extravagant spending and legal settlements. In 2008, Neverland Ranch, his famous estate, was nearly foreclosed. Jackson's health was also a subject of speculation, with rumors of skin conditions, plastic surgeries, and drug addiction frequently making headlines.

Amid these challenges, Jackson announced a comeback tour in March 2009 titled "This Is It," which was to consist of 50 concerts at the O2 Arena in London. The tour was highly anticipated, with tickets selling out quickly. Fans and the media viewed it as an opportunity for Jackson to reclaim his status as a top performer. However, the preparations for the tour added significant stress to Jackson's already fragile state.

On June 25, 2009, Michael Jackson was found unresponsive in his home in the Holmby Hills neighborhood of Los Angeles. His personal physician, Dr. Conrad Murray, attempted to resuscitate him before calling for emergency medical assistance. Jackson was rushed to the Ronald Reagan UCLA Medical Center, where he was pronounced dead at 2:26 PM. The news of his death was met with an outpouring of grief from fans, celebrities, and world leaders, highlighting his immense impact on global culture.

The immediate cause of Jackson's death was cardiac arrest, but the circumstances surrounding it soon led to a criminal investigation. The Los Angeles County Coroner's office conducted an autopsy and concluded that Jackson died from acute propofol and benzodiazepine intoxication. Propofol, a powerful anesthetic, is typically used in surgical settings and requires careful monitoring. The autopsy report also revealed that Jackson had several other medications in his system, including lorazepam, midazolam, diazepam, and lidocaine.

Dr. Conrad Murray, who had been hired to care for Jackson during the "This Is It" tour, admitted to administering propofol to Jackson as a sleep aid. The investigation revealed that Murray had been giving Jackson nightly doses of propofol for two months prior to his death. This practice was highly irregular and dangerous, as propofol is not intended for use as a sleep aid outside of a hospital setting. Furthermore, Murray failed to provide adequate monitoring equipment or take necessary precautions while administering the drug.

In February 2010, Murray was charged with involuntary manslaughter. The trial, which began in September 2011, focused on whether Murray's actions constituted criminal negligence. The prosecution argued that Murray's administration of propofol without proper safeguards directly led to Jackson's death. The defense contended that Jackson had self-administered an additional dose of propofol without Murray's knowledge, leading to a fatal overdose. The jury found Murray guilty, and he was sentenced to four years in prison, of which he served two years.

The trial and its aftermath did little to quell the myriad questions and theories surrounding Jackson's death. Some speculated that Jackson's own demands for powerful sedatives and his history of drug use were contributing factors. Others pointed to the pressures of his impending comeback tour and the stress of his financial situation. Jackson's complicated medical history, including his battles with chronic pain, insomnia, and anxiety, further complicated the narrative.

In the wake of Jackson's death, his estate faced legal battles and efforts to preserve his legacy. His mother, Katherine Jackson, and his three children, Prince, Paris, and Blanket, were at the center of these efforts. The estate's executors worked to settle debts and manage Jackson's assets, including his extensive music catalog. Despite the financial turmoil, Jackson's music continued to generate significant revenue, and his posthumous releases and merchandise remained popular.

Jackson's legacy as a groundbreaking artist is undeniable. His influence on music, dance, and popular culture is evident in the work of countless artists who followed him. His contributions to music videos and live performance set new standards in the entertainment industry. Songs like "Thriller," "Bad," "Smooth Criminal," and "Black or White" are timeless classics that continue to resonate with audiences around the world.

However, his legacy is also complicated by the allegations of child sexual abuse and the controversies that surrounded his personal life. Documentaries like "Leaving Neverland," released in 2019, brought renewed attention to the accusations against Jackson, with two men, Wade Robson and James Safechuck, alleging that Jackson had abused them as children. These claims reignited debates about Jackson's behavior and the impact of his actions on his legacy.

The death of Michael Jackson serves as a poignant reminder of the immense pressures and challenges faced by those in the public eye. His life was a testament to the heights of artistic achievement and the depths of personal struggle. The circumstances of his death, involving powerful medications and questionable medical practices, underscore the complexities of managing health and well-being in the context of celebrity.

As the years pass, Michael Jackson's contributions to music and culture continue to be celebrated, even as his life and death are scrutinized. His story is a multifaceted one, encompassing extraordinary talent, unprecedented success, personal tragedy, and enduring controversy. The world will remember him not only for his incredible artistry but also for the cautionary tale his life and death represent about the human cost of fame.

Chapter 42: The Mysterious Georgia Guidestones

The Georgia Guidestones, often referred to as "America's Stonehenge," are a granite monument erected in 1980 in Elbert County, Georgia. They have intrigued and baffled visitors and conspiracy theorists alike for decades. The monument consists of four large upright stones arranged in a paddlewheel configuration, with a capstone placed on top. One of the most enigmatic aspects of the Guidestones is the set of ten guidelines or principles inscribed on the stones in eight modern languages, including English, Spanish, Swahili, Hindi, Hebrew, Arabic, Chinese, and Russian. Additionally, a shorter message is inscribed at the top of the structure in four ancient languages: Babylonian cuneiform, Classical Greek, Sanskrit, and Egyptian hieroglyphs.

The origins of the Guidestones are shrouded in mystery. In June 1979, a man using the pseudonym R.C. Christian approached the Elberton Granite Finishing Company on behalf of "a small group of loyal Americans" and commissioned the structure. R.C. Christian claimed to represent an anonymous group that had been planning the monument for twenty years, aiming to create a guide for humanity in the event of a global catastrophe. Despite various theories about his true identity, the man known as R.C. Christian and his associates remain unidentified to this day, adding to the intrigue surrounding the monument.

The ten guidelines inscribed on the Guidestones have sparked considerable debate and speculation. The principles promote themes such as population control, environmentalism, and a new world order. They read as follows:

1. Maintain humanity under 500,000,000 in perpetual balance with nature.
2. Guide reproduction wisely—improving fitness and diversity.

3. Unite humanity with a living new language.
4. Rule passion—faith—tradition—and all things with tempered reason.
5. Protect people and nations with fair laws and just courts.
6. Let all nations rule internally resolving external disputes in a world court.
7. Avoid petty laws and useless officials.
8. Balance personal rights with social duties.
9. Prize truth—beauty—love—seeking harmony with the infinite.
10. Be not a cancer on the Earth—leave room for nature—leave room for nature.

The first guideline, calling for the maintenance of the global population under 500 million, has been particularly controversial. Critics argue that achieving such a population level would require a drastic reduction from the current global population, leading to speculation about the intentions behind this recommendation. Some interpret this as a call for a massive depopulation, possibly through catastrophic means, which has fueled numerous conspiracy theories about the true purpose of the Guidestones.

The second guideline advocates for guiding reproduction wisely to improve fitness and diversity. This has been interpreted by some as a call for eugenics, the controversial practice of selective breeding to enhance the human gene pool. The reference to a new living language in the third guideline has led to discussions about the creation of a universal language that could unite humanity, potentially replacing existing languages and cultures.

The principles encouraging fair laws, just courts, and the resolution of international disputes through a world court reflect ideals of justice and global governance. However, the idea of a world court has raised concerns among those who fear it could lead to a loss of national sovereignty and the imposition of a centralized, authoritarian world government. This feeds into the broader narrative of a "New World Order," a conspiracy theory that suggests a secretive global elite is working to establish an all-powerful, totalitarian regime.

Environmental themes are evident in the final two guidelines, which urge humanity to avoid being a "cancer on the Earth" and to leave room for nature. These principles have been interpreted as advocating for sustainable living and environmental conservation, which many view as positive and necessary. However, the ambiguous language and the association with the other, more controversial guidelines have led to suspicions about the true motivations behind these messages.

Adding to the enigma of the Georgia Guidestones are the astronomical features incorporated into their design. The structure is carefully aligned with celestial bodies. For example, a hole drilled through the center stone allows viewers to see the North Star, and a slot cut into another stone aligns with the sun's solstices and equinoxes. These features suggest that the Guidestones may have been intended to function as a type of modern-day astronomical calendar, further deepening the mystery of their purpose.

Over the years, the Guidestones have been the target of vandalism and have been defaced with graffiti espousing various conspiracy theories. This vandalism reflects the deep suspicion and controversy the monument has engendered among certain groups. Some believe the stones are part of a sinister plot by global elites to control or reduce the human population. Others see them as a harmless, albeit curious, monument advocating for peace, harmony, and environmental stewardship.

In addition to the physical structure and the inscribed guidelines, the Guidestones also feature an explanatory tablet set into the ground a short distance to the west of the monument. This tablet provides some context for the structure, though it raises as many questions as it answers. It mentions a time capsule buried beneath the tablet, but there is no date inscribed for when the capsule should be opened, leading to further speculation about what the capsule might contain and when it was intended to be unearthed.

The Guidestones have become a focal point for various conspiracy theories, ranging from the involvement of secret societies like the Freemasons or the Rosicrucians to connections with government agencies or wealthy elites. The anonymity of R.C. Christian and the group he represented fuels these theories, as does the enigmatic nature of the guidelines themselves. Despite the many theories, there has been no conclusive evidence to definitively explain who commissioned the Guidestones or why.

The Georgia Guidestones remain one of the most intriguing and mysterious monuments in the United States. Their blend of ancient languages, modern principles, and astronomical alignments continues to captivate and perplex those who visit them. Whether viewed as a benign guide for future generations, a sinister blueprint for global control, or something else entirely, the Guidestones stand as a testament to the enduring power of mystery and the human fascination with the unknown. As new generations discover the monument and interpret its messages, the legend of the Georgia Guidestones is likely to continue growing, ensuring their place in the annals of American lore and global conspiracy theories for years to come.

Chapter 43: The Illuminati's Influence in Hollywood

The idea of the Illuminati, a supposed secret society believed to control world events from the shadows, has permeated various aspects of popular culture, none more so than Hollywood. The influence of the Illuminati in Hollywood is a topic rich with speculation, theories, and accusations. This purported influence is said to extend to the highest echelons of the entertainment industry, encompassing actors, directors, producers, musicians, and other key figures who shape the narratives consumed by millions around the globe. According to these theories, the Illuminati utilizes its power within Hollywood to propagate its agenda, subtly indoctrinating the masses through movies, television shows, music videos, and other forms of media.

One of the primary reasons for the proliferation of these theories is the sheer visibility and influence of Hollywood celebrities. A-list actors and popular musicians have massive followings, and their behavior, statements, and artistic outputs are scrutinized by fans and critics alike. When these celebrities exhibit strange behaviors, make cryptic statements, or include symbolic imagery in their work, conspiracy theorists often interpret these actions as evidence of Illuminati affiliation. Symbols frequently cited include the All-Seeing Eye, pyramids, pentagrams, and other occult imagery, which are said to be hidden in plain sight within media content to subliminally influence viewers.

The origins of the Illuminati can be traced back to the Bavarian Illuminati, a secret society founded in 1776 by Adam Weishaupt. This organization aimed to promote Enlightenment ideals such as reason, secularism, and the separation of church and state. However, it was disbanded in the late 18th century under pressure from the Bavarian government. Despite this, the idea of a clandestine group manipulating world events persisted and evolved into the modern-day concept of the Illuminati. This group is often portrayed as a shadowy cabal of the world's most powerful individuals, including politicians, business leaders, and entertainment figures, working together to establish a New World Order.

In Hollywood, the purported influence of the Illuminati is often linked to the concept of mind control, particularly through a supposed program known as MK-Ultra. This program, originally a real series of experiments conducted by the CIA in the mid-20th century, aimed to explore the possibilities of mind control and psychological manipulation. Conspiracy theorists claim that remnants of MK-Ultra continue to operate within the entertainment industry, using celebrities as pawns to disseminate propaganda and condition the public. High-profile instances of erratic behavior among celebrities are often cited as evidence of MK-Ultra's ongoing influence. For example, public breakdowns, erratic behavior, and drastic changes in personality are interpreted as signs of mind control victims experiencing mental breakdowns due to the stress of their conditioning.

The music industry, in particular, is rife with Illuminati symbolism according to conspiracy theorists. Prominent artists like Beyoncé, Jay-Z, Lady Gaga, Kanye West, and Rihanna are frequently accused of being Illuminati members. Their music videos and performances are scrutinized for symbols and gestures that supposedly indicate their allegiance. For example, Beyoncé and Jay-Z's use of the "Roc" hand sign, which resembles a pyramid, is often cited as evidence of their involvement. Lady Gaga's theatrical and often bizarre performances are interpreted as displays of Illuminati influence, with her elaborate costumes and stage sets said to be filled with occult symbolism. Kanye West's frequent references to his alter ego "Yeezus" and his controversial behavior are seen by some as signs of his purported role within the Illuminati.

Movies are another medium through which the Illuminati is believed to spread its influence. Blockbuster films, with their wide reach and significant impact on popular culture, are seen as perfect tools for indoctrination. Theories suggest that Hollywood filmmakers embed Illuminati messages within their films, often through subtle symbolism or plot lines that reflect the group's alleged agenda. Films like "Eyes Wide Shut," directed by Stanley Kubrick, are often cited as prime examples. "Eyes Wide Shut" is filled with references to secret societies and elite gatherings, which conspiracy theorists believe reflect the real-life activities of the Illuminati. Kubrick's sudden death shortly after the film's completion only adds to the mystique, with some suggesting that he was silenced for revealing too much.

Superhero movies, with their themes of extraordinary individuals wielding immense power, are also frequently scrutinized. These films often depict shadowy organizations manipulating events from behind the scenes, which some interpret as a reflection of the real-life Illuminati. The Marvel Cinematic Universe, for instance, features several secretive groups such as Hydra and S.H.I.E.L.D., which are seen as analogs to the Illuminati. The idea is that these films condition viewers to accept the existence of such organizations and the notion of a powerful elite governing the world.

Television shows also come under scrutiny, especially those that achieve cult status or deal with themes of conspiracy and control. Shows like "The X-Files," "Stranger Things," and "Mr. Robot" delve into the idea of secret government programs and hidden truths, which are interpreted by conspiracy theorists as subtle revelations of the Illuminati's influence. The recurring theme of ordinary individuals discovering and battling against hidden forces resonates with those who believe in the existence of such a secret society.

The personal lives and public personas of Hollywood celebrities are another focal point for these theories. High-profile relationships, sudden deaths, and unexpected career changes are all viewed through the lens of Illuminati influence. The untimely deaths of stars like Michael Jackson, Whitney Houston, and more recently, Prince, have fueled speculation that these individuals were either members of the Illuminati who tried to break free or were victims of the society's machinations. Theories abound that these stars knew too much or posed a threat to the Illuminati's agenda, leading to their untimely demises.

Award shows, particularly the Grammy Awards and the Oscars, are seen as significant events for the Illuminati's public displays. Performances filled with elaborate and often controversial imagery are interpreted as rituals or messages from the society. For instance, Madonna's 2012 Super Bowl halftime show and Katy Perry's 2015 Super Bowl performance were both heavily analyzed for supposed Illuminati symbolism. These events are believed to serve as both celebrations of the society's influence and public rituals to reinforce its power.

Social media has played a crucial role in the spread and perpetuation of these conspiracy theories. Platforms like YouTube, Twitter, and Instagram provide a space for theorists to share their analyses and connect with like-minded individuals. Videos breaking down music videos, film scenes, and celebrity behavior for Illuminati symbolism garner millions of views, creating a feedback loop that perpetuates these ideas. Hashtags like #IlluminatiConfirmed trend periodically, further embedding the notion of Illuminati influence in the public consciousness.

While the concept of the Illuminati in Hollywood can be compelling and offers a way to make sense of the complexities and contradictions of the entertainment industry, it's essential to approach these theories critically. The entertainment industry, with its focus on creativity, spectacle, and pushing boundaries, often employs controversial or mysterious elements to generate buzz and attract attention. Symbolism and themes of power, control, and secrecy are common in storytelling and artistic expression, making them ripe for interpretation and misinterpretation.

Furthermore, the human tendency to seek patterns and connections can lead to seeing significance where none exists. The need to explain and rationalize the often unpredictable nature of celebrity behavior and the broader entertainment industry can make conspiracy theories particularly appealing. They provide a coherent narrative that simplifies the complexities of fame, creativity, and the pressures of the industry.

Despite the lack of concrete evidence supporting the existence of the Illuminati as a controlling force in Hollywood, the idea persists and evolves, reflecting broader societal anxieties and fascinations. Theories about the Illuminati offer a lens through which people can explore themes of power, control, and the unseen forces shaping their world. As long as there is a demand for such narratives, and as long as celebrities and media continue to captivate the public's imagination, the notion of the Illuminati's influence in Hollywood is likely to endure.

Chapter 44: The Secret Society of the Skull and Bones

The Skull and Bones, a secret society based at Yale University, has captured the imagination and curiosity of many due to its clandestine nature, influential members, and mysterious rituals. Founded in 1832, Skull and Bones is one of the oldest student societies in the United States. Its members, known as "Bonesmen," have included some of the most powerful and influential figures in American history, from presidents to Supreme Court justices, senators, and business magnates. This aura of secrecy and the prominence of its members have given rise to numerous conspiracy theories about the society's goals and influence.

The origins of the Skull and Bones society can be traced back to Yale students William Huntington Russell and Alphonso Taft, who established it as an elite organization. The society's emblem, a skull and crossbones, and the number 322 have become iconic symbols. The number 322 is believed to refer to the year of the society's founding or possibly to the death of the Greek orator Demosthenes in 322 BC, though its exact meaning remains a closely guarded secret.

Membership in Skull and Bones is highly exclusive. Each year, only 15 Yale seniors are "tapped" to join, making it an honor reserved for a select few. These new members are introduced into the society through elaborate initiation rituals that are shrouded in mystery. The initiation is said to involve bizarre and sometimes macabre rites, including confessions of personal secrets and the performance of rituals that bond the members together. While the specifics of these rituals are closely guarded, they are rumored to include the use of a human skull, hence the society's name.

The society's headquarters, known as the "Tomb," is a windowless, fortress-like building on the Yale campus. The Tomb is where the society conducts its meetings and rituals, and it is said to house various artifacts and memorabilia related to its history. The building's imposing architecture and lack of windows contribute to its aura of secrecy and exclusivity.

One of the most intriguing aspects of Skull and Bones is the notable individuals who have been members. Among them are three U.S. Presidents: William Howard Taft, George H.W. Bush, and George W. Bush. Other prominent members include Supreme Court justices, senators, and influential business leaders. The society's influence is often seen in the interconnectedness of its members, many of whom have occupied key positions in government, finance, and industry. This network of power and influence has led to speculation that Skull and Bones operates as a shadowy organization exerting control over American politics and economics.

The society's secrecy and the prominence of its members have given rise to numerous conspiracy theories. Some believe that Skull and Bones is part of a larger network of secret societies working towards a New World Order, a global government controlled by a small elite. These theories often link Skull and Bones to other secretive groups such as the Illuminati and the Bilderberg Group, suggesting a coordinated effort to control world events. The fact that many members of Skull and Bones have held influential positions lends some plausibility to these theories, though there is little concrete evidence to support them.

One of the most persistent conspiracy theories involves the supposed role of Skull and Bones in orchestrating major historical events. For example, some theorists claim that the society played a role in the assassination of President John F. Kennedy or in the planning of significant economic policies. These theories often hinge on the connections between Bonesmen and key figures involved in these events, though they typically lack definitive proof.

Another theory suggests that Skull and Bones has a significant influence on the CIA. This idea stems from the fact that several early members of the CIA, including its founder William Donovan, had connections to Yale and were rumored to be Bonesmen. Additionally, James Jesus Angleton, a prominent figure in the CIA, was a Yale graduate and reportedly associated with Skull and Bones. This connection between the society and the intelligence community has fueled speculation that Skull and Bones operates as a recruiting ground for future intelligence operatives, helping to shape U.S. foreign policy from behind the scenes.

The society's rituals and symbolism also contribute to the mystique and conspiracy theories surrounding it. The use of skulls, coffins, and other macabre imagery in its initiation rites has led to speculation about the society's true purpose and beliefs. Some theorists suggest that Skull and Bones engages in occult practices or has ties to ancient mystical traditions. These ideas are often fueled by the secrecy and exclusivity of the society, which leave much room for speculation and imagination.

In addition to its supposed influence on politics and intelligence, Skull and Bones is also thought to have a significant impact on the business world. Many Bonesmen have gone on to become leaders in major corporations and financial institutions, suggesting that the society serves as a network for advancing the careers of its members. This business influence is seen as another way in which Skull and Bones exerts control over American society, further fueling theories about its overarching power and reach.

The society's connections to prominent American families also add to its intrigue. For example, the Bush family has a long history with Skull and Bones, with both George H.W. Bush and George W. Bush being members. The Taft family, another influential American political dynasty, also has deep ties to the society. These family connections suggest a continuity of influence and power that spans generations, reinforcing the idea of Skull and Bones as a central node in a network of elite American families.

Despite the numerous theories and speculations, there is little concrete evidence to support the idea that Skull and Bones operates as a shadowy puppet master controlling global events. Much of what is known about the society comes from former members who have spoken out or from investigative journalists who have pieced together information from various sources. While these accounts provide some insight into the society's activities and influence, they often lack definitive proof of the more sensational claims made by conspiracy theorists.

The mystique of Skull and Bones is further enhanced by its portrayal in popular culture. Books, movies, and television shows have depicted the society as a secretive and powerful organization, often with nefarious intentions. For example, the 2000 film "The Skulls" is loosely based on Skull and Bones and portrays it as a society with a dark and dangerous influence. Such portrayals contribute to the public perception of Skull and Bones as a shadowy organization with significant, albeit hidden, power.

In reality, Skull and Bones is likely more of an exclusive social club than a nefarious cabal. Its members benefit from the networking opportunities and the sense of camaraderie that comes from being part of a prestigious and secretive society. The influence of Skull and Bones is more likely a result of the social connections and shared experiences of its members rather than a coordinated effort to control world events. However, the secrecy and exclusivity of the society continue to fuel speculation and conspiracy theories, ensuring that Skull and Bones remains a topic of fascination and intrigue.

The ongoing interest in Skull and Bones speaks to a broader human fascination with secret societies and the idea of hidden power structures. The society's combination of elite membership, mysterious rituals, and historical longevity make it a compelling subject for those interested in the hidden workings of power and influence. As long as there are unanswered questions and unexplained connections, Skull and Bones will continue to be a fertile ground for conspiracy theories and speculation.

Ultimately, the true influence of Skull and Bones is likely more nuanced and less sinister than many conspiracy theories suggest. While its members have undoubtedly held positions of significant power and influence, this is likely a reflection of the society's ability to attract ambitious and talented individuals rather than evidence of a coordinated effort to control global events. The allure of Skull and Bones lies in its mystery and exclusivity, and it is this aura that will continue to captivate the imagination of those who seek to uncover the secrets of the world's most powerful individuals.

Chapter 45: The Conspiracy of Chemtrails

The conspiracy theory of chemtrails is one of the most enduring and controversial in modern times. It posits that the trails left by aircraft in the sky, commonly referred to as contrails, are actually chemicals being deliberately sprayed for various nefarious purposes. These supposed purposes range from weather modification and population control to mind control and the spread of diseases. Despite widespread scientific refutation, the chemtrails conspiracy theory continues to attract a significant number of believers and has become a staple in discussions of government secrecy and environmental manipulation.

To understand the chemtrails conspiracy theory, it's important to first comprehend the phenomenon of contrails. Contrails, or condensation trails, are streaks of condensed water vapor created by the exhaust of aircraft engines at high altitudes. When the hot exhaust gases from jet engines mix with the colder, low-pressure air of the upper atmosphere, the water vapor in the exhaust condenses into tiny ice crystals, forming visible trails. These trails can persist for varying lengths of time depending on atmospheric conditions. In some cases, they dissipate quickly, while in others, they can linger and spread out, creating a veil of cloud-like formations.

Proponents of the chemtrails theory argue that these trails contain more than just water vapor and ice. They claim that governments and other powerful entities are using aircraft to disperse harmful chemicals into the atmosphere. The substances allegedly being sprayed include aluminum, barium, strontium, and other heavy metals, as well as biological agents and other toxins. According to this theory, these chemicals are intended to serve various sinister purposes, ranging from weather modification and geoengineering to mind control and population reduction.

One of the most commonly cited goals of chemtrails is weather modification. Proponents of the theory believe that the chemicals being sprayed are designed to manipulate weather patterns, potentially to combat climate change or to use weather as a weapon. This idea is rooted in historical attempts at weather modification, such as cloud seeding, where substances like silver iodide are dispersed into clouds to induce rainfall. While cloud seeding is a real and documented practice, the leap to widespread and covert chemtrail spraying lacks empirical evidence and scientific support.

Another alleged purpose of chemtrails is geoengineering, specifically solar radiation management. This involves reflecting sunlight back into space to cool the Earth and mitigate global warming. Some chemtrail believers argue that the substances being dispersed in the atmosphere are reflective particles designed to achieve this effect. However, while geoengineering proposals do exist in the scientific community, they are highly controversial, largely theoretical, and not implemented on a large scale. The claims of covert, large-scale geoengineering through chemtrails remain unsubstantiated.

The theory also posits more dystopian purposes for chemtrails, such as mind control and population reduction. Some adherents believe that the chemicals being sprayed have psychoactive properties designed to alter human behavior or reduce cognitive function, effectively controlling the population. Others argue that the chemicals are intended to cause illness and reduce the global population as part of a depopulation agenda orchestrated by a secretive global elite. These more extreme claims often overlap with other conspiracy theories involving government mind control programs, such as MK-Ultra, and population control efforts, such as those attributed to the Illuminati or other shadowy organizations.

The chemtrails conspiracy theory gained significant traction in the late 1990s and early 2000s, largely due to the proliferation of the internet and social media. Websites, forums, and social media platforms provided a space for like-minded individuals to share their observations, theories, and purported evidence. Photographs of persistent contrails, personal anecdotes, and speculative articles spread rapidly online, creating a community of believers who felt validated and supported in their views.

Prominent figures and public personalities have also contributed to the spread of the chemtrails theory. Some have used their platforms to promote the idea, lending it a veneer of credibility. For example, former U.S. Representative Dennis Kucinich included a reference to chemtrails in a proposed bill, the Space Preservation Act of 2001, although it was later removed. Public figures like these can amplify conspiracy theories by giving them exposure and a semblance of legitimacy.

Despite its popularity among certain groups, the chemtrails conspiracy theory has been widely debunked by scientists, meteorologists, and aviation experts. The scientific consensus is that contrails are a natural byproduct of aircraft engine exhaust and atmospheric conditions. Studies have shown that the substances found in contrails are consistent with the materials used in aviation fuel and the normal operation of jet engines. The presence of trace metals and other elements in the atmosphere can be attributed to various sources of pollution, not deliberate spraying.

Moreover, extensive analysis of air and water samples has failed to provide credible evidence of the high levels of aluminum, barium, and other chemicals that chemtrail proponents claim are being dispersed. Environmental agencies and research institutions have conducted numerous studies to address these concerns, consistently finding that the levels of these substances are within normal environmental ranges and are not indicative of large-scale atmospheric spraying.

The persistence of the chemtrails theory despite scientific refutation can be attributed to several factors. Cognitive biases, such as confirmation bias, play a significant role, as individuals are more likely to seek out and believe information that supports their preexisting beliefs. The internet and social media also create echo chambers where conspiracy theories can flourish unchecked by opposing viewpoints. Additionally, the complexity and invisibility of atmospheric science and aviation technology can make it difficult for laypeople to fully understand the phenomena they observe, leading to misinterpretation and suspicion.

The cultural and psychological appeal of conspiracy theories like chemtrails is also significant. They provide simple explanations for complex and often frightening phenomena, offering a sense of control and understanding. Believing in a grand conspiracy can also create a sense of belonging to a group with special knowledge, fostering community and identity among believers.

Efforts to debunk the chemtrails theory often face resistance and hostility from its adherents. Scientific explanations are sometimes dismissed as disinformation or part of the conspiracy itself. This distrust of official sources and experts is a common feature of many conspiracy theories, making it challenging to change the minds of those who are deeply invested in the belief.

The broader implications of the chemtrails conspiracy theory are also noteworthy. It reflects a deep-seated distrust of government and institutions, a hallmark of many contemporary conspiracy theories. This distrust can undermine public confidence in scientific research, environmental policies, and governmental transparency. In some cases, it can lead to real-world consequences, such as opposition to legitimate climate change initiatives or public health measures.

In recent years, the chemtrails theory has intersected with other conspiracy theories, such as those surrounding vaccines, climate change, and even the COVID-19 pandemic. This convergence of theories creates a complex web of beliefs that can be difficult to disentangle. For example, some individuals who believe in chemtrails also subscribe to the idea that vaccines contain harmful chemicals or that the COVID-19 virus was deliberately engineered. This interconnectedness can amplify the spread and impact of conspiracy theories, making them more pervasive and harder to counteract.

Despite the challenges, addressing the chemtrails conspiracy theory and similar beliefs is important for fostering a well-informed and rational public discourse. Efforts to educate the public about the science of contrails and atmospheric phenomena can help dispel misconceptions. Engaging with believers in a respectful and empathetic manner, rather than dismissing their concerns outright, can also be more effective in encouraging critical thinking and skepticism.

Ultimately, the chemtrails conspiracy theory is a testament to the enduring allure of secret knowledge and the human desire to understand and control the world around us. It highlights the need for clear communication of scientific concepts and the importance of fostering trust in institutions and experts. As long as there are unanswered questions and unexplained phenomena, conspiracy theories like chemtrails will likely persist, challenging our ability to distinguish fact from fiction in an increasingly complex and interconnected world.

Chapter 46: The Mysterious Death of Edgar Allan Poe

The mysterious death of Edgar Allan Poe, one of America's most famous and enigmatic writers, has fascinated and perplexed scholars, historians, and fans for over a century and a half. Poe's untimely demise in 1849 at the age of 40 remains shrouded in mystery and speculation, with numerous theories attempting to explain the circumstances surrounding his final days. His death is a fittingly dark and enigmatic end for a man whose work delved deeply into themes of death, madness, and the macabre.

Edgar Allan Poe was found in a state of delirium on October 3, 1849, in Baltimore, Maryland, outside a public house that was being used as a polling place for an election. He was discovered by Joseph W. Walker, a compositor for the Baltimore Sun, who reported that Poe was "in great distress, and... in need of immediate assistance." Poe was wearing clothes that were not his own, which was unusual and added to the mystery. He was taken to the Washington College Hospital, where he remained semi-conscious and incoherent, unable to explain how he had come to be in his condition. Poe lingered in this state for four days, during which time he reportedly called out repeatedly for "Reynolds," a person who has never been conclusively identified. He died on October 7, 1849, with his final words said to be "Lord, help my poor soul."

The immediate cause of Poe's death was recorded as "phrenitis," or swelling of the brain, but this was a catch-all term used at the time when the exact cause was unknown. The lack of a clear diagnosis and the strange circumstances of his discovery have led to a wide array of theories about what actually happened to Poe. These theories include alcohol poisoning, drug overdose, tuberculosis, epilepsy, rabies, carbon monoxide poisoning, heavy metal poisoning, murder, and a practice known as "cooping."

One of the earliest and most persistent theories is that Poe died as a result of alcoholism. Poe struggled with alcoholism throughout his life, a problem that was exacerbated by personal tragedies and professional failures. His bouts of heavy drinking were often followed by periods of abstinence, and he was known to be unable to handle alcohol well, often becoming violently ill after only a small amount. Some biographers have suggested that Poe's final binge led to his death, with the symptoms of delirium and confusion aligning with severe alcohol poisoning. However, there are inconsistencies in this theory. Poe had reportedly joined a temperance society shortly before his death and had been seen sober and healthy in the weeks leading up to his final disappearance. Additionally, no evidence of alcohol consumption was found in his system at the hospital.

Another theory posits that Poe may have died from drug overdose. It was rumored that Poe had a laudanum (a tincture of opium) addiction, but there is little concrete evidence to support this. His writings contain references to opium, leading some to speculate that he had personal experience with the drug. However, his medical records and the accounts of those who knew him do not strongly support the idea that he was a habitual user. Additionally, the symptoms he exhibited in his final days do not align neatly with those of an opium overdose.

Tuberculosis, a common and often fatal disease in the 19th century, is another possible cause of death. Poe's wife, Virginia, died of tuberculosis two years before Poe's own death, and he had experienced symptoms that could suggest the disease, such as chronic coughing and weakness. Some researchers believe that Poe may have contracted tuberculosis and that the stress and poor living conditions he experienced in the last months of his life exacerbated the illness, leading to his death. However, there is no definitive medical evidence to confirm this diagnosis.

Epilepsy is another medical condition that has been suggested as a cause of Poe's death. Some scholars have proposed that Poe suffered from temporal lobe epilepsy, which could account for his erratic behavior, periods of confusion, and possible hallucinations. The symptoms he exhibited in his final days, including altered mental status and incoherent speech, could align with a severe epileptic episode. However, epilepsy would not necessarily explain his disheveled appearance and the fact that he was found in someone else's clothes.

One of the more exotic medical theories is that Poe may have died from rabies. This theory was put forward in 1996 by Dr. R. Michael Benitez, who noted that Poe's symptoms were consistent with rabies: agitation, confusion, delirium, and hydrophobia (fear of water). Rabies also has an incubation period that fits with the timeline of Poe's final illness. However, there is no record of Poe being bitten by an animal, and rabies was not commonly diagnosed in humans at the time.

Carbon monoxide poisoning from coal gas, used for indoor lighting in the 19th century, has also been suggested. Chronic exposure to low levels of carbon monoxide can cause symptoms such as headaches, dizziness, confusion, and weakness, which could align with Poe's condition. However, this theory lacks direct evidence and is largely speculative.

Heavy metal poisoning, specifically mercury or lead poisoning, is another potential cause. Poe had a history of poor health and may have been exposed to various toxins throughout his life. Hair analysis of a sample from Poe conducted in 2006 revealed elevated levels of mercury, which could indicate poisoning. However, the levels were not high enough to be definitively fatal, and mercury poisoning typically produces a different set of symptoms than those Poe exhibited.

Murder is a theory that cannot be entirely ruled out given the chaotic and often dangerous environment of 19th-century Baltimore. Poe had many enemies and was known for his caustic literary critiques, which may have earned him animosity. Some speculate that he may have been the victim of a targeted attack or robbery, but there is no concrete evidence to support this, and his personal effects were found intact.

One of the most compelling theories is that Poe was a victim of "cooping," a form of electoral fraud common in the 19th century. Cooping involved kidnapping individuals, often vagrants or those deemed expendable, forcing them to vote multiple times for a particular candidate under different disguises, and often subjecting them to violence or intoxication to ensure compliance. Poe was found on Election Day near a polling place, and the fact that he was wearing clothes not his own suggests he may have been a victim of cooping. This theory aligns with the disoriented and distressed state in which Poe was found and provides a plausible explanation for the otherwise inexplicable circumstances.

The mysterious death of Edgar Allan Poe continues to be a subject of fascination and debate. The lack of definitive evidence and the various plausible theories have led to an enduring mystery that mirrors the themes of Poe's own literary work. His death, like many of his stories, is characterized by a sense of unresolved dread and ambiguity, leaving ample room for speculation and interpretation.

Poe's legacy as a master of the macabre and the mysterious is only heightened by the enigmatic circumstances of his demise. His work, filled with themes of premature burial, death, and madness, seems almost prophetic in light of his own unexplained end. The theories surrounding his death reflect the broader themes of uncertainty and fear that pervade his writing, making his life and death a continuous source of intrigue and study.

Chapter 47: The CIA's Involvement in Drug Trafficking

The topic of the CIA's involvement in drug trafficking is one of the most controversial and widely debated aspects of American intelligence history. Over the decades, numerous allegations have surfaced suggesting that the Central Intelligence Agency (CIA) has been complicit in, or directly involved with, drug trafficking operations around the world. These claims span various periods and geopolitical contexts, including Southeast Asia during the Vietnam War, Latin America during the Cold War, and the rise of the crack epidemic in the United States. Despite vehement denials from the agency and its defenders, these allegations have persisted, fueled by a combination of investigative journalism, declassified documents, and testimony from individuals involved in these operations. This discussion will delve deeply into the historical context, key incidents, and ongoing debates surrounding this contentious issue.

The origins of the CIA's alleged involvement in drug trafficking can be traced back to the early years of the Cold War. In the aftermath of World War II, the United States was deeply concerned with the spread of communism and sought to combat it through a variety of covert operations. The CIA, established in 1947, became a central player in these efforts, often allying with unsavory characters and organizations that could further its anti-communist agenda. In this context, the agency's relationships with drug traffickers were sometimes seen as a necessary evil to achieve larger geopolitical goals.

One of the earliest and most notable instances of the CIA's alleged involvement in drug trafficking occurred in Southeast Asia during the Vietnam War. The Golden Triangle, which includes parts of Burma (now Myanmar), Thailand, and Laos, was a major hub for opium production. During the 1960s and 1970s, the CIA supported anti-communist forces in this region, including the Hmong tribes in Laos, who were fighting against the communist Pathet Lao. According to various reports, including those by investigative journalist Alfred W. McCoy, the CIA facilitated the transport of opium to finance these operations. McCoy's book, "The Politics of Heroin in Southeast Asia," published in 1972, alleges that the agency was aware of and even protected drug traffickers who were aligned with its objectives. The book claims that the CIA's airline, Air America, was used to transport opium and heroin from the Golden Triangle to other parts of the world.

Another significant period where the CIA's involvement in drug trafficking has been alleged is during the 1980s, in the context of the Iran-Contra affair and the Contra War in Nicaragua. The Contras were a group of rebel fighters who opposed the Sandinista government, which had come to power in Nicaragua in 1979. The Reagan administration was determined to support the Contras despite a Congressional ban on further military aid. To circumvent this restriction, various covert operations were employed, including the sale of arms to Iran (itself a highly controversial move) and the diversion of the proceeds to fund the Contras. During this period, numerous reports and investigations suggested that the Contras were involved in drug trafficking, particularly cocaine, to finance their operations.

One of the most explosive claims came from investigative journalist Gary Webb, whose series "Dark Alliance," published in 1996 in the San Jose Mercury News, alleged that the CIA was complicit in allowing drug traffickers to smuggle cocaine into the United States. Webb's investigation focused on the connection between the Contras and drug dealers in Los Angeles, suggesting that the influx of cocaine contributed significantly to the crack epidemic of the 1980s. Webb's reporting indicated that the CIA turned a blind eye to these activities as long as the proceeds were used to support the Contras. His work provoked a firestorm of controversy, leading to widespread public outcry and demands for investigations. However, Webb faced significant backlash from mainstream media and government officials, and his work was discredited by many. Despite this, subsequent investigations, including those by the CIA's own Inspector General, confirmed some elements of Webb's reporting, acknowledging that the agency had contacts with drug traffickers and did not adequately report or stop their activities.

The allegations against the CIA are not limited to Southeast Asia and Latin America. In Afghanistan, following the Soviet invasion in 1979, the CIA provided substantial support to the Mujahideen fighters. Afghanistan has long been a major producer of opium, and during the 1980s, reports emerged that Mujahideen groups were heavily involved in the opium trade. Critics have suggested that the CIA turned a blind eye to these activities, prioritizing the fight against Soviet forces over concerns about drug trafficking. The long-term consequences of this period are evident in the enduring problem of opium production in Afghanistan, which remains a significant issue in global narcotics trafficking.

The complexity of the CIA's alleged involvement in drug trafficking is further compounded by the nature of intelligence operations, which often involve working with dubious characters and engaging in morally ambiguous activities. The necessity of secrecy and plausible deniability means that definitive evidence is hard to come by, and much of what is known comes from whistleblowers, declassified documents, and investigative journalism rather than official admissions. The CIA has consistently denied direct involvement in drug trafficking, arguing that any associations with drug traffickers were incidental and not indicative of an official policy.

However, several government investigations and hearings have explored these allegations, with varying conclusions. The Kerry Committee, led by then-Senator John Kerry in the late 1980s, investigated the connections between the Contras and drug trafficking, finding evidence that individuals associated with the Contras were indeed involved in drug trafficking, and that U.S. officials were aware of it. The CIA's Inspector General's reports, released in the late 1990s, similarly acknowledged that the agency had relationships with individuals involved in drug trafficking, though it stopped short of confirming direct complicity.

The broader implications of the CIA's alleged involvement in drug trafficking are significant. These allegations have fueled widespread distrust of the agency and the U.S. government, contributing to a perception of hypocrisy in the American war on drugs. Critics argue that while the U.S. government has aggressively pursued domestic drug enforcement policies, leading to mass incarceration and social disruption, it has simultaneously engaged in or tolerated drug trafficking abroad when it served its geopolitical interests. This double standard has had profound effects on U.S. foreign and domestic policy, as well as on the lives of countless individuals affected by drug addiction and violence.

Moreover, the legacy of these alleged activities continues to shape the geopolitical landscape. In Latin America, for instance, the destabilization caused by the drug trade and the associated violence has had lasting impacts on countries such as Colombia, Mexico, and Nicaragua. In Afghanistan, the opium trade remains a major challenge to stability and development, with narcotics funding insurgent groups and corrupt officials.

Chapter 48: The Government's Cover-Up of Bigfoot

The legend of Bigfoot, a large, ape-like creature said to inhabit the forests of North America, has captured the imagination of the public for decades. While many dismiss the idea of Bigfoot as a myth or a product of overactive imaginations, others fervently believe in its existence and contend that there is a vast government conspiracy to cover up evidence of the creature. This theory posits that the government has compelling reasons to suppress information about Bigfoot, including fears of public panic, the protection of natural resources, and the prevention of scientific upheaval. Exploring this topic requires delving into the history of Bigfoot sightings, the alleged evidence, and the supposed motives behind a governmental cover-up.

The modern Bigfoot legend can be traced back to the 1950s when a series of sightings and footprints captured public attention. The creature is often described as a large, hairy, bipedal humanoid, standing between 6 to 9 feet tall and weighing over 500 pounds. Its purported habitat includes remote forests and mountainous regions, particularly in the Pacific Northwest of the United States and Canada. Despite numerous reported sightings, photographs, and footprints, concrete evidence of Bigfoot's existence remains elusive, leading to speculation that the government is actively involved in concealing the truth.

Proponents of the government cover-up theory point to several pieces of alleged evidence to support their claims. One of the most famous pieces of evidence is the Patterson-Gimlin film, shot in 1967, which appears to show a large, bipedal creature walking through a forest in Northern California. While skeptics argue that the film is a hoax, many Bigfoot enthusiasts believe it to be genuine and argue that it represents undeniable proof of the creature's existence. However, the film has been subject to extensive scrutiny, with experts divided over its authenticity.

In addition to photographic and video evidence, there are numerous reports of physical evidence such as footprints, hair samples, and feces. Some researchers claim to have analyzed these samples and found them to be inconsistent with any known animal species, suggesting that they could belong to Bigfoot. However, critics argue that these samples are often contaminated or misidentified, and without a definitive DNA analysis, they cannot be considered conclusive proof. Despite this, believers argue that the government has the means and motive to suppress or discredit such evidence, further fueling the cover-up theory.

The government's alleged involvement in the Bigfoot cover-up is often linked to the supposed discovery of Bigfoot remains. According to some conspiracy theories, government agencies such as the FBI or the National Park Service have recovered bodies or skeletal remains of Bigfoot but have kept this information hidden from the public. These theories suggest that the remains are either destroyed or stored in secret facilities to prevent their discovery. Believers argue that such a cover-up is necessary to avoid public panic and the potential disruption to society that would come with the confirmation of Bigfoot's existence.

One of the main reasons cited for the government's desire to cover up the existence of Bigfoot is the potential impact on natural resources and the environment. Bigfoot is often reported in remote and pristine wilderness areas, which are also valuable for logging, mining, and other commercial activities. If Bigfoot were proven to exist, these areas might become protected habitats, leading to significant economic losses for industries that rely on exploiting these natural resources. The government, therefore, has a vested interest in keeping the existence of Bigfoot under wraps to avoid conflicts with powerful commercial interests.

Another motive for the cover-up is the potential impact on science and academia. The confirmation of Bigfoot's existence would have profound implications for the fields of biology, anthropology, and zoology. It would challenge established scientific theories about human evolution and the distribution of large mammals, leading to a paradigm shift in our understanding of these subjects. Such a discovery could also undermine the credibility of scientists who have long dismissed Bigfoot as a myth. To avoid this upheaval, the government and scientific institutions might prefer to suppress any evidence that contradicts the current consensus.

Additionally, the government might be concerned about the potential for public panic and the impact on tourism. National parks and wilderness areas are popular destinations for tourists, and the presence of a large, potentially dangerous creature could deter visitors. By covering up evidence of Bigfoot, the government can maintain the perception of these areas as safe and attractive destinations, ensuring a steady flow of tourism revenue.

Despite these alleged motives, there is also significant skepticism regarding the government cover-up theory. Critics argue that the lack of concrete evidence for Bigfoot's existence is more likely due to the creature being a myth or a case of mistaken identity rather than an elaborate conspiracy. They point out that the scientific community is generally open to new discoveries and that confirming the existence of a new species would be a major achievement, not something to be hidden.

Furthermore, the logistics of a widespread cover-up involving multiple government agencies, scientists, and officials would be extraordinarily complex and difficult to maintain. In the age of digital communication and whistleblower protections, it is increasingly challenging to keep such a significant secret hidden from the public. The lack of credible leaks or whistleblowers coming forward with undeniable proof of a cover-up also undermines the plausibility of the theory.

Despite these counterarguments, the belief in a government cover-up of Bigfoot persists among certain segments of the population. This belief is often reinforced by a broader mistrust of government and authority, as well as a fascination with conspiracy theories and the unknown. For many, the idea that the government is hiding the truth about Bigfoot is part of a larger narrative about the concealment of important information from the public, whether it involves UFOs, secret technologies, or other unexplained phenomena.

The enduring mystery of Bigfoot and the alleged government cover-up also highlights the cultural and psychological aspects of the phenomenon. Bigfoot serves as a symbol of the wild, untamed aspects of nature that remain beyond human control and understanding. The creature embodies a sense of wonder and mystery that is deeply ingrained in the human psyche. The idea that the government is hiding the truth about Bigfoot taps into this sense of mystery and the desire to believe in something greater and more mysterious than ourselves.

Moreover, the persistence of the Bigfoot legend and the cover-up theory speaks to the power of folklore and storytelling. Stories of large, hairy creatures have been part of human culture for centuries, with variations of the Bigfoot legend found in Native American folklore and other cultures around the world. These stories are often passed down through generations, evolving and adapting to new contexts and technologies. The modern Bigfoot legend, with its alleged government cover-up, is a continuation of this tradition, blending ancient myths with contemporary concerns about government secrecy and the unknown.

Chapter 49: The Secret of the Hollow Earth Theory

The Hollow Earth theory is a concept that suggests the Earth is entirely or largely hollow and may contain subterranean civilizations, environments, and even alternate worlds beneath its surface. This idea has intrigued and captivated the imaginations of many for centuries, blending scientific curiosity, speculative fiction, and conspiracy theories. Despite being widely dismissed by the scientific community, the Hollow Earth theory persists in popular culture and alternative science circles. Understanding this theory requires an exploration of its historical roots, the various interpretations and claims associated with it, and its cultural impact.

The origins of the Hollow Earth theory can be traced back to ancient civilizations and myths. Many cultures around the world have legends of underground realms and beings. For instance, the ancient Greeks spoke of Hades, an underworld ruled by the god of the same name, while Norse mythology features Svartálfaheim, a world inhabited by dark elves. These mythological concepts laid the groundwork for later speculative ideas about the Earth's interior.

The modern iteration of the Hollow Earth theory began to take shape in the 17th century. One of the earliest proponents was Edmond Halley, the English astronomer famous for Halley's Comet. In 1692, Halley proposed that the Earth consisted of a hollow shell about 500 miles thick, with two inner concentric shells and an innermost core. He suggested that these layers were separated by atmospheres and were capable of supporting life. Halley's theory was driven by his desire to explain anomalous compass readings and the Earth's magnetic field. Although his ideas were speculative and lacked empirical evidence, they captured the imagination of many thinkers of his time.

In the 18th and 19th centuries, the Hollow Earth theory gained further traction. John Cleves Symmes, Jr., an American army officer, became one of its most ardent advocates. In 1818, Symmes declared that the Earth was hollow and habitable within. He proposed that large openings at the poles, known as Symmes Holes, provided access to the inner world. Symmes even sought funding for an expedition to the North Pole to find these entrances, though he was unsuccessful in securing the necessary support. His ideas, however, continued to influence others, and the concept of a Hollow Earth persisted.

Literature played a significant role in popularizing the Hollow Earth theory. Jules Verne's 1864 novel "Journey to the Center of the Earth" is perhaps the most famous literary work inspired by this concept. In the story, Professor Lidenbrock and his companions descend into an Icelandic volcano and discover a vast underground world filled with prehistoric creatures and other wonders. Verne's novel, though fictional, sparked public interest and added a sense of adventure and mystery to the Hollow Earth idea.

Another significant literary contribution came from Edward Bulwer-Lytton, whose 1871 novel "The Coming Race" describes a subterranean civilization possessing advanced technology and psychic abilities. The inhabitants, called Vril-ya, live in vast underground cities and utilize a mysterious energy source known as "vril." Bulwer-Lytton's work influenced later esoteric and occult interpretations of the Hollow Earth theory, particularly in the late 19th and early 20th centuries.

In the 20th century, the Hollow Earth theory found new life through the writings of figures like Willis George Emerson and Richard E. Byrd. Emerson's 1908 novel "The Smoky God" tells the story of Olaf Jansen, a Norwegian sailor who supposedly discovered an inner world inhabited by giants. Jansen's account, presented as a true story, added a layer of supposed authenticity to the Hollow Earth narrative.

Admiral Richard E. Byrd, a pioneering American aviator and explorer, is often cited in Hollow Earth literature due to his polar expeditions. In 1947, Byrd allegedly flew over the North Pole and reported seeing a lush, green land with lakes and rivers. Some Hollow Earth proponents claim that Byrd's observations support the existence of an inner world. However, these claims are based on disputed accounts and lack corroborating evidence. Byrd's documented expeditions do not support the Hollow Earth theory, but his name is frequently invoked in discussions on the topic.

The Hollow Earth theory also intersects with various esoteric and occult traditions. In the early 20th century, some Theosophists, followers of the spiritual movement founded by Helena Blavatsky, embraced the idea of subterranean realms inhabited by advanced beings. They linked the Hollow Earth concept to their broader cosmology, which included ancient civilizations like Atlantis and Lemuria. The idea of hidden masters or ascended beings living beneath the Earth's surface became a recurring theme in esoteric literature.

During the same period, Nazi Germany's interest in the occult and pseudoscience led to speculation about their involvement in Hollow Earth research. Some conspiracy theories suggest that the Nazis conducted secret expeditions to the poles in search of entrances to an inner world, possibly seeking advanced technology or alliances with subterranean civilizations. While there is little credible evidence to support these claims, they have contributed to the enduring mystique of the Hollow Earth theory.

The concept of the Hollow Earth continues to appear in modern popular culture. Science fiction and fantasy authors frequently explore the idea of hidden worlds beneath the Earth's crust. For example, Edgar Rice Burroughs' "Pellucidar" series, beginning with "At the Earth's Core" (1914), depicts a prehistoric world inside the Earth inhabited by dinosaurs and primitive humans. More recently, films like "Journey to the Center of the Earth" (2008) and video games like "Hollow Knight"

(2017) draw on the rich tradition of subterranean adventure inspired by the Hollow Earth theory.

Despite its enduring popularity in fiction and conspiracy theory circles, the Hollow Earth theory is not supported by scientific evidence. Advances in geology, seismology, and geophysics have provided a detailed understanding of the Earth's structure. The Earth consists of a solid inner core, a liquid outer core, a viscous mantle, and a solid crust. This layered structure is supported by extensive seismic data, which show how seismic waves travel through different materials within the Earth. These observations are consistent with a solid, not hollow, interior.

Seismic waves generated by earthquakes provide a wealth of information about the Earth's interior. When these waves travel through the Earth, they behave differently depending on the type of material they encounter. By studying the speed and path of seismic waves, scientists have been able to map the internal structure of the Earth with great accuracy. The presence of a solid inner core and a liquid outer core, as well as the properties of the mantle and crust, are well-established through these methods.

Additionally, gravitational measurements and observations of the Earth's magnetic field support the conventional model of the Earth's interior. The distribution of mass within the Earth affects its gravitational field, and these measurements are consistent with a solid, layered structure. The Earth's magnetic field, generated by the movement of molten iron in the outer core, also aligns with the accepted understanding of the Earth's internal composition.

While the scientific consensus firmly rejects the Hollow Earth theory, it remains a captivating idea for many. The allure of hidden worlds and undiscovered civilizations taps into a deep-seated human fascination with the unknown. For some, the Hollow Earth theory represents a challenge to mainstream scientific thought and a symbol of alternative knowledge. The theory also reflects broader cultural and psychological themes, such as the fear of what lies beneath the surface and the desire for exploration and discovery.

214

Chapter 50: The Mystery of the Zodiac Killer

The Zodiac Killer is one of the most infamous and mysterious serial killers in American history, responsible for a series of brutal murders that terrorized Northern California in the late 1960s and early 1970s. The killer's identity remains unknown, and the case has inspired numerous books, films, and theories, contributing to its enduring allure. The Zodiac Killer not only committed heinous crimes but also engaged in a psychological game with the public and the media, sending taunting letters and cryptic ciphers to newspapers, further deepening the mystery and intrigue surrounding the case.

The Zodiac Killer's reign of terror began on December 20, 1968, with the murder of high school students Betty Lou Jensen and David Faraday in Vallejo, California. The couple was parked in a secluded area on a date when they were approached by an unknown assailant. Faraday was shot once in the head, and Jensen was shot multiple times in the back as she tried to flee. The brutal nature of the crime shocked the local community, but it would soon become apparent that this was just the beginning of a series of horrific acts.

The next confirmed attack occurred on July 4, 1969, when Darlene Ferrin and Michael Mageau were shot while sitting in Ferrin's car in a parking lot in Vallejo. Ferrin was killed, but Mageau survived despite being shot multiple times. He later provided a description of the shooter, although it was not detailed enough to lead to an identification. Shortly after the attack, the killer called the Vallejo Police Department from a payphone, confessing to the crime and linking it to the earlier murders of Jensen and Faraday.

The Zodiac's most notorious crime occurred on September 27, 1969, at Lake Berryessa in Napa County. Bryan Hartnell and Cecelia Shepard were picnicking by the lake when they were approached by a man wearing an executioner's hood and a bib-like garment with a cross-circle symbol, which would become the Zodiac's signature mark. The assailant tied them up and brutally stabbed them before leaving the scene. Despite their injuries, Hartnell survived and was able to provide a detailed description of the attacker, though Shepard succumbed to her wounds a few days later.

Just two weeks later, on October 11, 1969, the Zodiac struck again in San Francisco, killing cab driver Paul Stine. This time, the killer deviated from his usual pattern by targeting an adult male and committing the murder in an urban setting. Stine was shot in the head at point-blank range, and the Zodiac took a piece of the victim's bloodied shirt as a trophy. Witnesses saw the killer leaving the scene, and a police sketch was created based on their descriptions.

Throughout his killing spree, the Zodiac Killer taunted authorities and the public by sending a series of letters to local newspapers, including the San Francisco Chronicle and the Vallejo Times-Herald. These letters often included ciphers, which the Zodiac challenged readers to decode, claiming that they contained his identity. The first of these ciphers, sent in three parts to different newspapers in July 1969, was cracked by a schoolteacher and his wife. It read: "I like killing people because it is so much fun. It is more fun than killing wild game in the forest because man is the most dangerous animal of all." Despite this disturbing confession, the cipher did not reveal the killer's name.

The Zodiac's letters continued to provide tantalizing clues and unsettling threats. He often included details about the murders that were not publicly known, further establishing his credibility. In some letters, he claimed to have killed more people than the confirmed victims, suggesting that his true body count might be much higher. The Zodiac also threatened to attack school buses and kill children, causing widespread panic and leading to increased security measures.

One of the most enduring mysteries of the Zodiac case is the remaining unsolved ciphers. Of the four ciphers sent by the Zodiac, only one has been definitively solved. The most famous unsolved cipher, known as the 340-character cipher (Z340), remained a mystery for over 50 years. In December 2020, a team of amateur codebreakers announced that they had cracked the Z340 cipher using sophisticated computer algorithms and pattern recognition techniques. The decoded message did not reveal the killer's identity but reiterated his enjoyment of killing and his disdain for authorities.

Numerous suspects have been investigated over the years, but none have been definitively linked to the Zodiac crimes. One of the most prominent suspects was Arthur Leigh Allen, a convicted child molester and former schoolteacher. Allen was first identified as a suspect in 1971 and was linked to the case through various circumstantial evidence, including his possession of a Zodiac watch bearing the killer's symbol and statements he made to friends about killing people. Despite extensive investigation, no conclusive evidence was found to directly tie Allen to the murders, and he died in 1992 without being charged.

Another notable suspect was Richard Gaikowski, a journalist who worked for an underground newspaper in San Francisco. Gaikowski's behavior and writings during the time of the Zodiac murders raised suspicions, and some researchers believe his physical appearance matched the police sketch of the Zodiac. However, like Allen, there was no definitive evidence linking Gaikowski to the crimes, and he died in 2004.

The Zodiac case has also attracted a plethora of amateur sleuths and conspiracy theorists, each with their own theories about the killer's identity and motivations. Some believe the Zodiac was a highly intelligent and organized individual who managed to evade capture through meticulous planning and manipulation of the media. Others suggest that the Zodiac may have had military or law enforcement experience, given his knowledge of ciphers and his ability to avoid detection.

In addition to the confirmed victims, the Zodiac Killer is suspected of involvement in several other unsolved cases. These include the murders of Robert Domingos and Linda Edwards in 1963, the death of Cheri Jo Bates in 1966, and the disappearance of Donna Lass in 1970. While there are similarities between these cases and the confirmed Zodiac murders, definitive links have not been established, and they remain speculative.

The cultural impact of the Zodiac Killer is significant. The case has been the subject of numerous books, documentaries, and films, including David Fincher's 2007 movie "Zodiac," which dramatizes the investigation and its impact on those involved. The Zodiac's taunting letters, cryptic ciphers, and the unresolved nature of the case have contributed to its status as one of America's most enduring true crime mysteries.

The continued fascination with the Zodiac Killer can be attributed to several factors. The killer's use of ciphers and coded messages adds an element of intellectual challenge and intrigue, inviting people to try their hand at solving the puzzles. The brutality and randomness of the crimes, combined with the killer's ability to evade capture, create a sense of fear and uncertainty. Additionally, the lack of closure and the possibility that the killer could still be alive contribute to the enduring allure of the case.

Despite decades of investigation and advances in forensic science, the Zodiac Killer remains unidentified. DNA evidence, which has solved many cold cases, has not yet provided a breakthrough in the Zodiac case. In recent years, there have been efforts to use modern DNA analysis techniques, such as genetic genealogy, to identify the killer. This approach, which was famously used to capture the Golden State Killer, involves comparing DNA from crime scenes with public genealogy databases to find relatives of the suspect. While these efforts have not yet yielded results, they offer a glimmer of hope that the Zodiac's identity may eventually be uncovered.

Epilogue

As we reach the conclusion of "Mysterious Conspiracies: The Secret Plots of History," we stand at the intersection of fact and fiction, where the shadows of doubt intertwine with the light of understanding. Through these chapters, we have traversed a landscape of enigmatic events, powerful secret societies, unexplained phenomena, and haunting mysteries that continue to captivate the minds of truth-seekers and skeptics alike.

Each conspiracy we have explored serves as a testament to the human spirit's insatiable curiosity and the desire to uncover hidden truths. These stories remind us that history is not always a straightforward narrative but a complex tapestry woven with threads of intrigue, deception, and the unknown. They challenge us to question the official accounts, to look beyond the surface, and to seek out the stories that lie beneath.

While some of the conspiracies we have examined may never be fully resolved, their enduring allure lies in the very mystery that surrounds them. They provoke thought, spark debate, and invite us to consider alternative perspectives. In a world where information is power, these tales remind us to remain vigilant, to question authority, and to never stop searching for the truth.

As you close this book, consider the broader implications of these conspiracies. They are more than mere curiosities; they are reflections of our societal fears, our mistrust in institutions, and our quest for knowledge. They reveal the lengths to which individuals and groups will go to protect their secrets and the resilience of those who seek to expose them.

In the end, the true power of these conspiracies lies not in the answers they provide but in the questions they raise. They challenge us to think critically, to remain open-minded, and to recognize that the world is often more complex and mysterious than it appears. Whether you are a believer or a skeptic, the stories within these pages serve as a reminder that history is an ever-evolving narrative, shaped by the interplay of truth and deception.

Thank you for embarking on this journey through the secret plots of history. May it inspire you to continue exploring the unknown, to seek out the hidden truths, and to never stop questioning the world around you. The search for understanding is a never-ending quest, and the mysteries of the past are but stepping stones to the discoveries of the future.

The End.